DESERT RIMS to
MOUNTAINS HIGH

DESERT RIMS to MOUNTAINS HIGH

Richard Francis Fleck

WESTWINDS
PRESS®

THE PRUETT SERIES

Text © 2004, 2013 by Richard Francis Fleck

Some of the essays in *Desert Rims to Mountains High* were originally published in *Breaking Through the Clouds* by Pruett Publishing, 2004.

Library of Congress Cataloging-in-Publication Data
Fleck, Richard F., 1937-
  Desert rims to mountains high / Richard Francis Fleck.
    pages cm — (Pruett series)
  Includes bibliographical references and index.
  ISBN 978-0-87108-968-7 (pbk.)
  ISBN 978-0-87108-982-3 (e-book)
  ISBN 978-0-87108-986-1 (hardbound)
  1. Mountaineering—West (U.S.) 2. Natural history—West (U.S.) 3. West (U.S.)—Description and travel. 4. Fleck, Richard F., 1937—Travel—West (U.S.) I. Title.
  GV199.42.W39F55 2013
  796.5220978—dc23
                    2013017957

Cover photo: © iStockphoto.com/David Parsons

Interior Design: Jean Andrews
Cover Design: Vicki Knapton

WestWinds Press®
An imprint of

GRAPHIC ARTS
BOOKS®

P.O. Box 56118
Portland, Oregon 97238-6118
503-254-5591
www.graphicartsbooks.com

CONTENTS

For my wife, Maura,
our children Rich, Michelle, Maureen, and their families,
who shared many a trail with me.

ACKNOWLEDGMENTS

I WISH TO ACKNOWLEDGE Pruett Publishing Company (now incorporated by Graphic Arts Books), the original publisher of a smaller version of this book entitled *Breaking Through the Clouds* (2004).

Additional chapters including the earlier versions of the Prologue, Descent into History at Grand Gulch, Adventures Below Desert Rims, Descent into the Grand Canyon, Climbing Windy Guadalupe Peak, Particles of Desert Sand, and the Epilogue originally appeared in an earlier out-of-print book *Where Land Is Mostly Sky* (Passeggiata Press, 1997), in the journals *Trail and Timberline, Colorado Outdoors,* and online sites www.suite101.com and www.hubpages.com.

Two publishers have anthologized sections of the book:

"The Solace of Dinosaur Ridge," in *The Landscape of Home,* ed. Jeff Lee. Boulder: Johnson Books, 2006.

"The Pefect Kiva," in *Stories and Stone,* ed. Reuben Ellis. Tucson: University of Arizona Press, 1997.

PROLOGUE:
DEATH VALLEY

WHAT'S STOVE PIPE WELLS going to look like? The map didn't do much for me in a Denver sporting goods store months before our planned visit. Would there be diamondback rattlers, tarantulas, and scorpions? Not in March, I supposed. And yet I well remembered a diamondback rattler one late spring day in New Mexico. My friends called him "The General." He pretty much had his way until that day when he climbed the screen door of their house out in the desert near Pena Blanca. That was too much, but they didn't want to kill him, they just shouted and screamed at him till he slid down to the ground and slithered off toward a field of yuccas.

My whole family including my wife, Maura, our children, and their spouses met in Las Vegas, Nevada, from all the corners of America. Why Las Vegas? I had to give a paper there at a convention but promised we would leave (after playing a few slots) for Death Valley, California, to the northwest to a place called Stove Pipe Wells. Would this be a hole-in-the-wall on flat, hot sand? Would there be any vegetation at all? I had read about desert bighorn sheep and wondered if we would see any there. Why Stove Pipe Wells?

Well, back in that sporting goods store in Denver, I read a brief description of Mosaic Canyon just outside of Stove Pipe Wells—that consists of a serpentine marble, smooth slickrock, dry waterfalls, bighorn sheep and, generally, cobalt blue skies.

As we raced northward beneath Mount Charleston outside of Las Vegas, a disturbing desert-brown floater suddenly appeared in the corner of my left eye. A year earlier my retina had detached, but my operation to repair it was successful. Was my eye falling apart again as we approached the Valley of Death? I let no one know of my discomfiture—didn't want to spoil the trip. (Later I found out my retina was fine, but a harmless tiny brown floater—a little piece of the desert—had begun to float around in my vitreous humor.) Finally, Beatty, Nevada, came into sight, and our turnoff for Death Valley, the continent's deepest geologic fault line. We climbed up to a pass at 4,000 feet, and there was Death Valley, a narrow, winding, white valley with wrinkled, elephant-skinned mounds rising here and there—"hills like white elephants" as Hemingway wrote about the landscape of Spain. On the downsloping hillsides sprouted occasional pinyons, junipers, yuccas, desert poppies, and cotton-top cactus amid an array of colorful stones gleaming in the sun. We stood in the Funeral Range and across from us rose the Panamints, and above them the high and snowy Sierra. I couldn't help but think of Frank Norris's character McTeague floundering around with his bird cage in the middle of Death Valley.

I told my family to chin up even though we had no rod or staff to comfort us. Down, down we went until we reached the five-mile-wide valley fault line to witness landscapes as poetically barren as those of Georgia O'Keeffe. Ravens circled overhead in a cloudless sky. Waves of sand spread northward and rugged canyons loomed westward like pieces of Mars. We had become giddy with energy and laughed and giggled constantly—so much the better for me as my worries and concern over my eye dissipated like clouds over the desert. "Well, I'll be . . ." said I as we approached the green oasis of Stove Pipe Wells nestled in the shade of willows and cottonwoods, a cute little town that blended into Death Valley as though it really wasn't there.

Lunch eaten, we drove up a gravel road to the trailhead of Mosaic Canyon. A desert fox trotted across the road ahead of us into mesquite bushes in pursuit of water or small game or both, his tongue dangling. The sandy entrance to Mosaic Canyon rose above beckoning us to experience lands unknown. Shouldering our packs, eight of us hoofed across sands into the serpentine canyon with a steady cool wind blowing into our faces. Bright yellow desert poppies fluttered in the wind along the trail that narrowed down to single-file width. We twisted and turned through smooth slickrock impregnated with occasional bands of sandstone conglomerates. Reds, browns, grays of rock bore down on us the deeper we ventured. Green mesquite bushes, yellow and white poppies, pickle-green pickleweed, and arrowroot tried to bloom in this very arid desert that had received lower than normal rainfall last winter.

Once atop a series of ledges, we peered across to the distant Mesquite Dunes, white against the blueness of sky. Later we would frolic on these rippled piles of sand surrounded by dark and wrinkled canyon-lands rising abruptly to the west and east. In the spirit of fun, we all bounded up a parallel trail, my son Rich leading the way, until we came to a knife-edge dirt ridge. Soon the drop-off down into Mosaic Canyon became so severe that my daughters Michelle and Maureen became frightened. I suggested they turn around slowly and backtrack to the main trail to rejoin my wife, Maura. Easier said than done! With trepidation, each turned slowly to get down on their haunches and slide the rest of the way down to the lower trail. Nerves recovered, they quickly joined the rest of us at the trail junction after we had descended a steeper, more difficult route.

Arriving at a dried-up waterfall, my wife and youngest daughter, Maureen, decided to rest with a supply of water and snacks while the six of us (including my son, oldest daughter, sons-n-law and daughter-in-law) continued upward through chimneys and chutes until we reached the top of the dry falls to see more of Mosaic Canyon rising forever above reds and browns and layers of conglomerates looking like some giant, grooved brain petrified by desert winds. On another day in the future we hoped to complete the twenty-six mile trail up into one of these grooves. We swilled some cool canteen water and looked and looked for bighorn sheep—nary a one was to be seen—just circling ravens above and gray lizards scampering on the rocks at our feet, but one of them stretched itself to sunbathe. No small coincidence that the French verb "to sunbathe" is *lezarder*. Each of us sat on a chosen perch and peered into the desert lands of Death Valley for who knows how long. Though we kept our silence, we remained very much a family unit, flecks of consciousness amid rock and space.

Death Valley's stark beauty is too vast to be borne by one individual alone; it must be shared. A writer attempts to share. I tried to imagine this valley at dawn's early light in layers of pink and then red and then gold. I tried to imagine dying here in Death Valley. Would it be death at all, or a transformation into the essence of the desert? But thoughts of death gave way to thoughts of life, a rich life with my wife and children and their mates. Death Valley brought us together in ways only each of us may fully know.

One by one we arose from our semi-meditative states and began our descent to the other family members. Luckily no snakes, only fast scampering lizards. As had been explained by the store owner in Stove Pipe Wells, poisonous reptiles keep their distance from the scent of humans, particularly they keep their distance from a well-used trail. Amazingly, a cool March wind refreshed us by rushing up-canyon, just the reverse of its down-canyon rush at the beginning of our hike, as if we had ordered it.

Soon we joined my wife and youngest daughter and merrily descended toward the dunes, stopping to watch a thirsty coyote lap water from a spring. He was terribly thirsty and continued to drink as we drove on down to Stove Pipe Wells where we stopped for cold bottles of sparkling water and soon drank as heartily as that coyote. The man at the shop suggested we should drive to the lowest point in the western hemisphere (282 feet below sea level) and walk out onto the shimmering and caked salt flats. He didn't have to twist our arms. Though I started to worry about my eye again, I thought that if I must go blind, there was no better place than here to remember my last visual impressions of God's good Earth. With all its wrinkled landscapes and shimmering mirages, Death Valley contained the very planetary essence of the Great American West.

1

DESCENT INTO HISTORY AT GRAND GULCH, UTAH

A PETROGLYPHIC LAYERING of thin, white clouds spread over Utah's Grand Gulch southwest of Blanding. Some took the shape of fuzzy, horned mountain goats and others writhing serpents which soon shed their wispy skin. The scent of pine and juniper permeated bone dry air as our group of twelve trudged deeper into Kane Gulch, a tributary of the Grand Gulch. Forty-pound packs ground into our shoulders with each jarring step downward past snapping branches of sagebrush and willows. The sound of a tiny, trickling stream to our left made me thirsty and the dust from twelve pairs of marching boots even thirstier. It didn't take long, however, to begin to gain a feel for this place with its scents and sounds, especially the trilling of canyon wrens and the melodious notes of the western song sparrow. We stopped for a rest on cool and dark slickrock in a hollow of the descending stream, its icy waters carrying young willow leaves in peaceful rhythm to lower valleys. I hadn't quite expected so much vegetation in this part of Utah. Each species of tree—whether a Gambel oak, a willow, or a cottonwood—had its distinct shade of green.

"What color are those trees, kid," asked my grandfather as he looked up from his easel in Philadelphia's Fairmont Park. "Green," said my mother who was then a small child. "Look again, kid," he said as he dabbed his brush in a rich variety of greens.

Within an hour's hoof from this hollow of greenness, we reached the Junction Ruins (at the junction of the Kane and Grand Gulches) under a sky of woven cotton clouds. This small Anasazi (Ancestral Puebloan is now preferred) sandstone village stood alone under an overhanging cliff erasing time a thousand years. Points of pottery shards stuck out of the sandy soil leading up to the ruins. Most of the pieces appeared to be rough with a corrugated texture, almost as rough as the miniature corn cobs tossed away centuries ago. The sight of small handprints painted on the smooth cliff walls testified to the former presence of these people who seemingly left only weeks ago. In fact, they hadn't left at all what with the smell of soot on the plastered sandstone slab walls, the sight of well-worn indentations left by grinding implements on the soft rock, and the presence of strands of yucca fiber rope, which they may have used to lower pots of corn down to the cliff dwelling from fields above. Life, not death, prevails over these ruins. It is life's force that made this place, and that force is present ever so abundantly.

After we snacked and drank some water, one member of our party suggested moving on to Turkey Pen Ruins to set up camp for the night. The few more miles along the trail proved to be both fragrant and musical. Golden hollygrape flowers, smelling like Mormon honey, attracted hummingbirds and western meadowlarks that translated the highs and lows of the surrounding rock walls with commensurate notes. Desert varnish graced all of the gulch's cliffs with finger-shaped stains of black, gray, red, and white.

Who cared about the pain in our shoulders from those ridiculously heavy packs? John Muir had it right, though—hike only with bread crumbs, tea leaves, and matches. But the Grand Gulch is not Muir country by a long shot, and we were hungry for more than bread crumbs.

What did these ancient people feed on who lived here eight hundred years ago? Corn definitely. Turkeys? Perhaps they penned wild turkeys more for their feathers (used for sleeping mats) and for eggs than for their meat. Beans and squash for sure, not to mention pinyon pine nuts and wild strawberries. They certainly hunted mountain goats, mule deer, and rabbits as the bones of these animals have been found in their ancient trash heaps. They built up appetites as strong as ours by carefully constructing sandstone dwellings, storage chambers, and ceremonial kivas; by climbing up and down sandstone hills to farm the mesa tops; and by occasionally hunting wild game.

Plodding along our trail, we were refreshed by the sight of flowers: bright red scarlet gillia, yellow clusters of Rocky Mountain bee plant, and chili pepper–red firecracker penstemon faintly suggesting bowls of hot chili!

Had similar swallows' nests made out of mud hanging throughout the canyon inspired the Anasazi to do likewise? Perhaps hornet nests inspired them as well. Modern day Native Americans tell us that each animal has something to teach human beings. Spiders weave, coyotes always look back over their shoulder, hummingbirds cross-fertilize squash blossoms, and owls hunt at night when small mammals are most active.

At last we came to an incredibly lush bend in the valley with a curving arch of sandstone cliffs rising above the Turkey Pen Ruins. Twilight had settled in as our cookstoves hissed away like serpents; some of us gourmandized on couscous, others on tortillas and beans, and still others on spaghetti. It had become too dark to climb the cliffs up to the ruins which gave us the excuse to sit back and listen to a nighttime chorus of frogs, owls, and jays. For a moment I thought I was back in South Florida's Corkscrew Swamp where the evening is hardly silent but alive with the piping of creatures large and small. We could readily imagine that these sounds came from the spirits of the protective chindi hovering around the ruins keeping away alien intruders. Who knows what I dreamed of that night under the glow of a full moon.

White cliffs glinted in the rising sun giving contrast to the dark hollow housing Turkey Pen Ruins. A quick breakfast in our bellies and we climbed to the ruins across a high, sandy ridge beneath the overhanging sandstone. Slowly we approached an enclosure of tightly knit willow branches whose shadows slanted across the sand. No doubt about it—a turkey pen with small piles of petrified golden-brown dung. We half expected to see wild turkeys clucking loudly trying to chase us away. As if to anticipate our coming, the ancient ones had painted images of turkeys both standing and sitting on the cliff walls behind the pen. Quiet though it was, you couldn't help but sense the presence of these people and their penned turkeys.

We climbed with care to an upper house high on a ledge above the turkey pen. The masonry, the ceiling, the jutting pinyon pine logs remained perfectly intact. We looked closely at the masonry to see rough sandstone slabs cemented together with mud mortar and stone chips for leveling. Clearly the masonry of this upper dwelling was a work of art as were the ceilings made of willow branches and smooth plaster.

The view from the inside to the outer world was stupendous—first a curving arch of woven sandstone looking like a tan sky, and then the blue sky itself above the winding river valley lush with vegetation, and finally the far side of the valley bending with its own sandstone cliffs; the whole valley indeed appeared to be a great ceremonial kiva. Three or four of us, including my son Rich, and Reuben Ellis, the college instructor of the others from Hope College, Michigan, sat here for an hour just staring and listening. Voices from more of Reuben's students talking below seemed to merge with the stone, sounding like they were next to us. Space in this valley also bent around the contours of sandstone cliffs. The Turkey Pen Ruins proved Einstein right; time and space combine to make here there and there here. Above all, our perspectives on life changed. Whose civilization lay in ruins? The ancient ones? It depends on how you define ruins.

Rich and I climbed a little higher to get a closer view of pictographs portraying a series of winged people with little fingers coming from the tips of wings. Perhaps they were representations of bat people; we certainly had seen a bat or two flicking past our candle lantern the previous evening. These bat-like pictographs constituted a fair percentage of the Turkey Pen Ruins rock art.

Above these creatures was a mystery: Four white thimble-shaped pictographs in a square pattern seemed to float in space. Just below and to the right were four more sets of them in a straight line. Under these white, thimble-like objects were eight slanting lines (four in each row), a bat-like person, and two crescent moons with horns facing upward. Perhaps the white thimbles represented the spirits of bats. These pictographs, whatever they are, strongly possess the presence of mind and spirit in a specific place.

Tom Outland, Willa Cather's fictionalized representation of Richard Wetherill (modern discoverer of the Mesa Verde ruins) says it well: "I cared more about them [Anasazi people] than about anything else in the world. . . ." They "belonged to boys like you and me, that have no other ancestors to inherit from." Tom, an American orphan, uses the word "belong," I believe, in a spiritual sense. Like Tom Outland, we all felt that we had somehow become familiar with these ancient ones, and, perhaps, they had become familiar with us. I got the distinct impression that time here is not a one-way street; places like this allow those from the past to come forward, and when they do, our spirit's core is never again quite the same.

Our trail companions from below gathered together with us on the upper ledge above our campground to sit and listen to frogs, crickets, mourning doves, and a lone canyon wren trilling with its endless highs and lows. I hated to leave this place, but we had miles to go before arriving at the next site, the Split Level Ruins.

Thunderheads gathered as we broke camp. Would these clouds bring rain? For the ancient ones rain was ever-so essential. Ceremonial life centered around rain clouds and spirits who gathered rain clouds. Rain could never be taken for granted; it must be prayed for in earnest. The day after next we would visit the Perfect Kiva Ruins to explore physical space set aside for such ceremony. Each and every ceremony was quintessential for survival. If rain did not come, was the sincerity of a people at fault? Why did these people leave Grand Gulch? Why did others leave the more urban settlements of Mesa Verde and Chaco Canyon? Where are they now?

Extensive drought in the late 1200s (determined by tree ring analysis) might serve as a partial answer. Extensive drought must have meant extensive prayer and extensively unanswered prayer might well account for their departure. Late twentieth-century clinical analysis of such factors as soil depletion, crop failure, and corresponding dietary insufficiency may also help answer the question. The unwitting lowering of the desert water table through over-utilization of trees for timber (especially at sites like Chaco Canyon) may serve as yet another answer to the question, why did they leave?

Are they still here? might be answered by the presence of the ceremonial kiva in today's Pueblo villages in the moister, snow-fed Rio Grande Valley of New Mexico. A Taos elder once told me, beneath the snowy slopes of Mount Wheeler, that oral tradition explains that the people of Taos came from Bandelier's Frijoles Canyon in north-central New Mexico, and the people of Bandelier may have come from drought-stricken Chaco Canyon (northwestern New Mexico), and the people of Chaco may have come from places like Mesa Verde and the Grand Gulch. Are these oral traditions in any way plausible? Yes, judging from the variety of pottery samples that trace back to original locations. But all this is conjecture. Still, ardent prayer for rain is very much part of modern day Pueblo Indian culture, even if there is seemingly abundant water. Nothing whatsoever must be taken for granted. Years ago I visited Sandia Pueblo near Albuquerque during a ceremonial dance for corn to mature. We watched intently as generations of people from young children to parents and grand-parents to even great grandparents danced for rain in the heat of midday. Oh how they danced! They devoted their entire beings to supplicate for rain, even if only a few drops of rain.

We could have stood a few drops of rain as we trekked in dry, ninety-degree heat past white and gnarled trunks of ancient junipers, the very type of junipers that reminded Edward Abbey of his stubborn father. Nary a cloud was there in the sky down in this part of the canyon.

Anxious to move on quickly, my son Rich and I forged ahead of the group through sagebrush thickets. Suddenly my son raised his hand nervously. When

I caught up with him, he said "didn't you see the diamondback rattler winding his way back and forth next to our trail?" Though I hadn't seen the serpent, just the thought of him brought Emily Dickinson's striking poem to mind:

> A narrow fellow in the Grass
> Occasionally rides—
> You may have met Him—did you not
> His notice sudden is—
> The Grass divides as with a Comb—
> A spotted shaft is seen—
> And then it closes at your feet
> And opens further on—
> But never met this fellow
> Attended, or alone
> Without a tighter breathing
> And Zero at the Bone—

Zero at the bone describes our feeling perfectly—at least until we arrived at a runoff pool, an oasis of ice water amid an increasingly desert-like canyon. Waiting for the arrival of our trail companions, I waded up to my knees into this Icelandic pool following a sandbar around to the back of a small waterfall where green mosses coated the rocks and cliff.

It was all I could do to get back to the starting point so numb were my feet, a rather pleasant feeling, nonetheless, for being in the midst of a hot desert. When the rest of the hiking partners arrived, one of the Hope College kids immediately stripped to the waist and plunged into the pool. As he surfaced, he couldn't form words on his lips so cold was this mid-May water. He waded back to the beach like someone who had fallen overboard in the Arctic Ocean, too cold to say "Wow!" We told others of our snake sighting and to be careful as we ever-so-gingerly proceeded one mile farther to the Split Level Ruins nestled high in a cool sandstone hollow.

Our tents formed a circle among an ancient stand of junipers as old as the Split Level Ruins themselves. If the ancient ones believed in the communal link of all living things including trees, one could ask, did the Anasazi really ever leave? If the juniper, bat, wren, owl, serpent, firecracker pensemon, were truly part of their village, part of their being, then one could say a part of these people is still here. I suspect we do feel the tug of the spiritual fusion of humans with flowers, mountain sheep, and buzzing flies even if this fusion comes from more remote planes of existence. Petroglyphs and pictographs assist in our sensing a lingering presence. These places foster the union of various planes of existence like no other location on Earth. Here is truly the Rocky Mountain Time Zone, a mythological zone whose minutes click by with centuries attached to them.

Despite the trickle of a small stream nearby, our campsite proved to be distinctly drier and more desert-like than the night before. But with water (purified by our filters) in good supply and a plethora of food, we experienced no hardships whatsoever, except for having to climb a steep hill up to the ruins.

Split Level Ruins is a marvelously preserved piece of architecture in two levels with perfect willow-branch ceilings and firmly mortared walls housing numerous chambers. Each and every breeze coming from the valley below or cliffs above wafted through these buildings creating a perfect summer air conditioning. These sandstone slabs surely absorbed winter sunrays and held them through the night to furnish these ancient people of over eight hundred years ago with indirect solar warmth. The acoustics up here proved to be ideal for listening to nature's perpetual concert of frogs, birds, crickets, and wind in the willows. The swoosh of a raven's wings in the sky above almost made me duck. Crickets hundreds of yards away sounded like they chirped in the kiva (their underground ceremonial chamber) below our feet.

"Hey Dad, look over here," said Rich. He had crawled inside a smoky room built right into the bottom of the sandstone cliff. He peered out the narrow doorway all smiles. "Can still smell the smoke from their cooking," he said. "In fact, it's making me hungry." The sun lingered brightly on the higher cliffs as the valley darkened below. Lizards scampered in search of warmer rocks.

Our descent to camp below led us past Spanish bayonets and green yucca spires whose roots furnished the Anasazi with fibers for such articles as sandals and rope. Soon we cooked our meal of dehydrated honey-lime chicken and mopped our steaming plates with homemade chili-pepper bread. Coffee and cookies finished things just right. Reuben invited us over to his campfire surrounded by his students to discuss desert literary classics, this time Ann Zwinger's poetic *Wind in the Rock* (1978). It was neat to sit by a fire and listen to the students' insight, but we couldn't help but look up at all the glittering stars above. On our way back to our tent, we listened in silence to the plaintive notes of a pair of mourning doves who seemed to speak to us from another world, certainly not ours.

Split Level cliff glowed bright red in the rising sun. Today we had to cover eight miles in desert heat with those stubborn forty-pound packs all the way to our last site before departing the Grand Gulch. Carefully handling a steaming mug of coffee, I plodded back up to Split Level Ruins for one last look. Pottery fragments, some orange, some black, some black and white peppered the sandy soil. How did they bake these clay vessels? They probably burnt bright-flaming juniper branches in a narrow sandstone alcove. That would certainly bake clay all right, but I wonder if they might not have used wild turkey dung also for the same purpose. You can see the results of Anasazi potters in museums throughout the Southwest. They are incredibly beautiful vessels with patterns of black and white squares and occasional representations of curved lizard figures for handles.

As others awakened from a mummy-like sleep down below, I figured we would be breaking camp soon. There remained eight, long, hard miles to go to get to our next site. Would we encounter more snakes? Would we spot unnamed ruins? Would all twelve of us maintain our energy levels?

Eight miles in ninety-degree heat created difficulties for all of us. We burnt through water quickly and the bouncing backpacks chafed our shoulders.

Thankfully no yellow-eyed serpents reared their heads to give us a feeling of zero at the bone. We did spot numerous unnamed dwellings balanced precariously on narrow little ledges half hidden in shadows giving credence to the observation that all of Grand Gulch in southeastern Utah served as a gathering place for isolated, rural Anasazi communities unlike the more urban sites at Mesa Verde and Chaco Canyon.

In the heat of noon we paused for snacks on a rocky spillway of a small stream, though hardly anyone was hungry. I barely noticed a stranger—an older, very tan, blond-haired woman munching on some trail mix; some of us struck up a conversation with her. After several minutes of chitchat she announced she must leave because she (like Greta Garbo) treasured solitude. She slithered off into the willows with only a day pack and disappeared forever. Some of us thought she vanished even before she reached the trees—too much exposure to the sun or to Tony Hillerman novels, no doubt.

We lingered a moment longer listening to caroling birds seemingly un-bothered by the ferocious heat. Perhaps they sang from the shade of deeply rooted Gambel oaks or from well within the willow thickets where the old woman had vanished. Perhaps they were the old woman herself singing in solitude. We followed after her and soon we, too, disappeared into the thicket.

After three days and three nights of exploring, we descended Grand Gulch toward the San Juan River before we could proceed up into Bullet Canyon, our exit canyon that would lead us back up to the world of the rim. At the lowest point it seemed even hotter, but why were the willows getting so thick down here in the valley? we wondered. We rested frequently in any shady grove we could find and praised the Great Spirit when we at last arrived at the mouth of Bullet Canyon, a tributary of Grand Gulch. We came across some campers who warned us that water was extremely scarce here, but we might find a few springs near the Perfect Kiva.

Our trail rose rapidly and with each foot gained in elevation, we enjoyed what we thought was cooler air. The higher we trudged with forty-pound packs, the easier it seemed. Passing under Jail House Ruins (with jail-like wooden bars in the windows), we knew we had but a half mile to go to procure filtered water from tiny springs and set up camp for the last time on this trip through time. We selected a high ledge of slickrock a few hundred yards from the Perfect Kiva. My son Rich and I chose a sandy spot within the slickrock to pitch our tent. Others did the same in the waning hours of the day. Having to break camp early the next day, some of us grabbed our flashlights for a nighttime exploration of this last of the Anasazi sites containing a perfectly preserved kiva. Stumbling along the dark and dusty trail with my flashlight, I recalled nighttime climbers scampering up the sacred slopes of Mount Fuji (Fuji San) in hopes of greeting the rising sun bobbing over the Pacific Rim.

Just a few pinyon jays studded the nightscapes below us in a more arid and stark landscape than the previous sites. When the last of our group arrived at the level terrace housing the Perfect Kiva Ruins, we individually explored these dark dwellings, shined lights on eerie petroglyphs, and eventually each of us descended the ladder to the underworld.

The world of the kiva is a world of its own. My descent into this Earth's womb at nighttime on an upper ledge above Bullet Canyon brought me back to pre-Columbian times—perhaps even to mythological times. All history is mythology wrote Henry Thoreau. If one goes back far enough in time, human history blurs with mythological traditions. Contemporary Southwestern tribal people believe that humans emerged from a lower spirit world in ancient times. All spirits pass through a small entrance to and from that spirit world called a sipapu. According to modern day Pueblo people, the original grand sipapu is at the mouth of the Little Colorado River just before it joins the Colorado River in the Grand Canyon. It is in the form of a small volcanic cone that rises through and above deep sandbars.

All of today's Pueblo villages up and down the Rio Grande have kivas with sipapus stemming back to Anasazi times. For a moment or two in the darkness of this womb, I imagined a stream of souls coming from and going to this earthly life. The womb seemed like a clearinghouse, and anyone alive in bodily flesh would have to be reminded of the transience of human existence. Do we have enough corn to eat? Are my springs plentiful? Will it rain? All these questions are put into perspective inside a kiva.

Many have conjectured on pre-Columbian activities in a kiva. One Native American ranger at Mesa Verde National Park suggested several years ago that a priest or shaman may have danced by firelight upon a wooden foot drum, and he may have chanted to his people the story of human emergence from the lower depths. He may have preached the necessity of maintaining natural harmony through prayer and ceremony. Without prayer there would be no rain. Without concern for the entire village, one person may reap undo benefits from Nature. Heya, hey hey! I almost heard the shaman sing. Time for me to climb out and let others experience the world of the kiva.

It was utterly amazing to see the luminescent sandstone glowing in starlight far below. Where was I? Still on this Earth? As others emerged from the kiva's depths, we gradually regrouped and sat in silence staring into space. Each of us, in his own way, had been very far away, and each of us had to come back. One person in our exploratory group thought he might have seen the pinyon pines inching along the sandstone floor; he wasn't back yet from the other world.

After carefully picking our way downslope and getting water from a lower spring, we were ready for sleep in the comfort of our tents. But not yet! Just as we unrolled our sleeping bags, a strange light appeared on the rimrock above us. Were we still in the kiva? What on earth was going on? Then a big arc of light rose over the canyon rim right next to the strange bright light. Earthly reality reformed itself into the rising of the moon and Jupiter, father of the planets. The moon gradually illuminated a semicircular sandstone cliff across the way from our camp as though some grand theater would soon take place. The moonlight emphasized each crack in the cliff as though it were exposing some ancient hieroglyphic language. The Perfect Kiva attuned each of us to the nature beyond nature, and we were thankful. We slept soundly that night somewhere between here and there.

2

ADVENTURES BENEATH DESERT RIMS

I—Keet Seel

EVER SINCE JOHN SULLIVAN and I had passed a warning sign on our way to Betatakin Ruins in Navajo National Monument, Arizona, we knew we must make the nine-mile hike into Keet Seel Ruins. The warning read, "This arduous trail to Keet Seel is open only to seasoned hikers who register in advance." Once back at the visitor center, we received an instruction booklet on the Keet Seel hike. The trail is closed during the winter months and registration is absolutely required for hikers who are in good shape. Each hiker is required to bring two gallons of water (that's seventeen pounds of extra weight!), because Navajo cattle graze streamside all along the canyons up to Keet Seel. Nonetheless both John and I registered for a hike to Keet Seel the following April before the intense heat of summer. We were also required, on the evening before our hike, to take a one-hour orientation class at the visitor center.

That winter we did some brainstorming on how to deal with two gallons of water each. A lightbulb suddenly lit up! We decided to put water in plastic quart jugs that would be spray-painted, each with a bright orange stripe. Instead of lugging seventeen pounds of water all the way to Keet Seel campground, we would each drop a quart bottle every two miles in an easily seen spot so that our weight would gradually disappear every two miles on the way in. We would still have sufficient water along the way and at our final destination. But we would have no water to carry on the way back! Every two miles we would have a quart of cool water each. For food, we would carry dehydrated meals and fruit/nut snacks.

April finally arrived and we packed our supplies and tents and sleeping bags and drove on down to Navajo National Monument, Arizona, not too far south of the Utah border outside of Kayenta. The visitor center is above 7,000 feet and our canyon hikes would be some thousand feet lower. We met our Keet Seel guide, Patrick Joshevama, a Hopi Indian ranger, at the visitor center the evening before our hike. He explained one other difficulty that we would encounter on our hike; the well-marked trail (with white posts) crisscrosses a very muddy stream perhaps forty or fifty times. Be aware of quicksand that gathers around the base of large boulders. It is simply best to avoid going anywhere near these boulders. Make sure, he said, to get an early start before 5 or 6 A.M. in order to arrive before the heat of the afternoon sun. He mentioned that he would be leaving for his post at Keet Seel around 5 A.M. We were to be the first hikers of the season and we would be among a group of less than eight hundred hikers per year from the entire planet!

We woke up from our tents just a little too late to catch Patrick on his hike into Keet Seel. We left an extra gallon jug of water in the car for our return the next day and trekked off to Tsegi Point (where the warning sign is) at 7,280 feet. It was precisely 6 A.M. on a pleasantly cool morning in late April. We began our descent of 1,000 vertical feet into Tsegi Canyon past juniper, pinyon pines, Gambel oaks, and box elders. The scant forest had a few April flowers growing here and there including Rocky Mountain bee plant, scarlet gillia, and rosy Indian paintbrush. With the steepness of this zigzagging trail, we thought it best to place an orange striped bottle beneath an old juniper tree halfway down. Red and tan sandstones cliffs on both sides of Tsegi Canyon dominated the desert landscapes. Already the temperature had risen by, perhaps, ten degrees. Too bad we missed Patrick at 5 A.M. when it was even cooler. A canyon wren trilled as we reached the bottom of Tsegi Canyon where we would follow, every half mile or so, white posts marking the trail.

Once down in Tsegi Canyon we had to cross Tsegi Creek and faithfully took off our boots and waded across. We followed the trail for about a mile and finally located the white post marking the entrance to Keet Seel Canyon; we had about six miles to go and 600 vertical feet to gain up to the ruins themselves. Shortly after passing the junction we placed two more quart bottles of water in a cool recess off the trail. But I'll be darned if the trail didn't come up to an abrupt canyon wall forcing us to cross muddy Keet Seel Creek. We noticed cattle tracks up to the creek's edge on the other side where we put our boots back on. After about the third time, though, we said to ourselves, what the heck; we may as well keep on the boots (mine were brand-new) to cross and recross this stream. Sometimes our feet got stuck in deep, gooey mud, and it was all we could do to get out of the mud trap. Each time we crossed, our boots got muddier and muddier and wetter and wetter and heavier and heavier. Patrick Joshevama was right about having to cross and recross this stream some fifty times one-way. Reg Saner had it right in his book *Reaching Keet Seel*: The adventure of reaching Keet Seel is just that, reaching it. Everett Ruess (who perished in the canyons of the Southwest) worked on an archaeological excavation at Keet Seel in the early 1930s. He mentions in his letters that he, too, became bogged down in quicksand on a "bad trail" to Keet Seel.

By the time we arrived at the first of three waterfalls, the desert began to enter deep into our psyche. Turquoise-blue skies with puffs of cloud, rising red sandstone walls, the bellowing of an occasional Navajo cow, gliding hawks high above, the sound of a shallow gurgling stream, the rising temperature all added a touch of desert to the inner being whether the hiker is trail-weary or not. The first waterfall tumbled about fifty feet with the trail skirting up and around the edge of the white water with its soothing mist. At the third set of falls, we somehow lost the trail and hoofed a half mile up into a box canyon before we realized our mistake. Back down we came weaving our way through stands of rabbitbrush until we found our trail that had been obscured by a large rock. We just had two more return-trip water bottles to place along the trail side and where huge black, square chunks of boulders came to the creek's very edge is exactly the spot where we each dropped a bottle to the ground. We were within two miles of Keet Seel campsite and on a broad stretch of the upper Keet Seel stream where we placed our last return bottle. Up here we would have several bottles left in our packs for use at the campsite and for hiking up to the ruins with Patrick.

Before meeting up with our guide, we hoofed up a steep side trail to the campsite (having about eight spaces) deep in a grove of rustling oak trees. After setting up our tents, each of us stretched out to doze off for thirty winks. Since it was now late afternoon, we went up to Patrick's summer hogan to let him know we were ready for the short, guided hike up into Keet Seel at last. Patrick soon led us through some oak woods to the base of the hollow cliff housing the ruins. We learned that Keet Seel is a Navajo term for "broken pottery," and, indeed, broken pottery lay scattered all around the base of the cliff; some of the larger shards were eye-catching with fantastic patterns of black on white. We then proceeded up a seventy-five-foot ladder into an ancient small city that spreads over 120 yards with living quarters, kivas, storage chambers, and meat-smoking rooms. Keet Seel housed 150 people between AD 950 and 1300 when a drought forced them to evacuate. Standing up there, we stared in wonder at the fine masonry of sandstone slabs and incredibly intricate, woven willow-branch ceilings. Patrick showed us the painstaking method they used to weave together their ceilings with yucca fiber reinforced with turkey-feather quills pinned inside of the fiber! Having recently visited Chaco Canyon, I asked our guide if the people of Keet Seel spread turquoise powder on the ground before they placed sandstones on top to construct walls as a kind of spiritual assurance. Patrick simply said that has not yet been determined. We walked past Anasazi pots lining the earthen walls along with grinding stones used for making corn mash bread or making hot gruel to drink on a cold winter's day. We caught the strong scent of smoke wherever we stood listening to Patrick.

He showed us several turkey pens (similar to those in the Grand Gulch) to reiterate the source of turkey quills for ceiling construction. Their feathers and eggs were of most importance. He pointed down to their spring which, up until the drought, furnished them with fresh cold water. The spring, along with rainwater, helped create muddy seeps where corn, beans, and squash grew in abundance. They used the "three sisters" method of growing crops with tall corn stalks in the middle, beans beneath, and prickly-vined squash at the outer edges that kept away harmful insects. What the corn took out of the soil, beans put back in. Patrick became quiet for a moment and then shared with us the fact that these ancient ones were his ancestors. His group of Hopi came up from Mexico to settle in Arizona and he felt that, as with his people, clans were of extreme importance. In fact, some sets of living quarters here at Keet Seel were walled off from others indicating the division of clans such as the bear clan, the coyote clan, and the fire clan. Patrick believed that the fire clan (keepers of the fire) had a strong presence in Keet Seel as they do with the Hopi at Shongopovi.

He furthered mentioned that these ancient ones were far from being vegetarian as they supplemented their diet with elk and deer meat often made into jerky for the long months of winter. They were herbalists and made use of many different plants for human ailments. For instance, if an ancient one accidentally cut himself, he would get sap or pitch from a pine tree to place it on his wound and stop the bleeding. He could make delicious wild tea from such things as serviceberry and the green stalks of Mormon tea that contained ephedrine. As we descended the ladder to the valley below, hawks circled the sky and an owl hooted in the distance. Patrick invited us into his hogan where we sat down on a comfortable couch and looked up at the Native American art gracing the walls. He brewed a fresh pot of coffee and shared biki or Hopi blue cornflake bread in very thin chips which were delicious.

That night, I decided to sleep out of my tent under the brilliant array of stars seen through the swaying oak branches. I felt a kinship with the ancient ones as I, too, so appreciated stars over the desert. After a nice, peaceful sleep, we left bright and early the next morning to retrieve our cool untouched water bottles every two miles on the way back up a long, tiring, dusty trail to Tsegi Point and our car.

II—Ute Mountain

A year later John Sullivan, Jim Ledbetter, and I planned ahead to have a Ute Indian guide lead us through the Ute Mountain Reservation side of Table Mesa that also houses Mesa Verde National Park. As we drove into the Ute tribal trading post, we knew we would be in for a walking tour of some pretty rugged country below the Table Mountain rim. Once our guide, Marshall, arrived, we and two other groups of people followed him into the Mancos Valley to a trailhead that led 1,000 vertical feet straight up to Two-Storey Ruins. He explained to us all, standing in a circle, that we should have a gallon of water each, and an extra jacket or sweater for the much cooler rim at almost 8,000 feet, and to be on the lookout for three dangerous creatures: rattlesnakes, mountain lions, and black bears, during our eight-mile trek. He warned us that a mountain lion can see you an hour before you see him. But he said not to worry as he would be carrying a loaded shotgun should a lion make an appearance. Bears tended not to confront a whole group of people.

We shouldered our day packs with several plastic bottles of water, trail snacks, and a modest lunch. Today would be exploring three ruins all within the Ute Rez. We immediately began a very steep ascent through a pinyon pine and juniper forest. Just as we all began to huff and puff, Marshall stopped to point out cheat grass to us growing along the side of the trail. It got its name from cheating other plants out of much-needed water. Clumps of gray-green sagebrush and stalks of cholla cactus spouted up a safe distance away from cheat grass. Onward and upward we raced once again toward our first objective, Two-Storey Ruins, that soon came into view. We all, thankfully, rested by stretching out on sandstone ledges below the ruins surrounded by scores of sharp-pointed yuccas whose pods can be eaten when ripe in autumn. Marshall called them "Navajo bananas." Cliff swallows buzzed around like chindi spirits protecting this ancient residence from intruders.

We each got up to explore the grain storage chamber and look at the upper story of these ruins built in AD 1130. We all followed Marshall up Moki steps in the slanting sandstone cliffs to the second-floor dwelling quarters and looked out through windows to the Mancos River gently flowing 800 feet below. Marshall explained that the Ute people were originally a mountain tribe who dwelt high in the Rocky Mountains of Colorado and Utah but were forced, in 1897, by the US government to live way down in the desert of the Four Corners region in a location called Ute Mountain Reservation which, surprisingly, contained many of these ancient ruins. The Utes, he emphasized, do not claim the Anasazi to be their ancestors like the Pueblos and Hopis. Since we still had a number of miles to cover, Marshall raised his hand up in the air and slowly lowered his arm pointing upward for us to climb still higher to the very rim of Table Mesa where we would be able to visit the Hoot Owl Ruins just shy of 7,000 feet.

Arriving at the base of a crooked wooden ladder set at a weird angle, one by one we climbed while trying to avoid remaining straight (as one ordinarily would) by leaning sideways until all of us stood high on the white capstone rim in a cool and steady breeze. From here we could see the La Plata Range, still white with snow, to the northeast. We sat in a circle to eat our lunches and sip water and ask Marshall some questions. "If not the Pueblos or Hopis, what tribes are culturally the closest to Utes?" Jim Ledbetter asked. "Definitely the Shoshone of northern Wyoming and Idaho. We can almost understand their language sort of like a Frenchman in Italy," Marshall replied. "Do you still get together in powwows?" I asked. "We may have when we both hunted in the mountains of northern Colorado and southern Wyoming," he said. He then stood up and swayed his arm in the direction of the edge of the rim.

Marshall explained that the next set of ruins is a bit more difficult to reach. "You're gonna have to descend some steep Moki steps to get down to Hoot Owl Ruins built in the early 1100s." Those of us in our late sixties and early seventies elected not to go. But the young folks eagerly followed Marshall to the edge. Then suddenly he descended, facing outward on the steps from below the cliff as though he were taking a department store escalator down. On his way down, he said that "you all don't have to go down this way. It's probably safer for you to turn around facing into the cliff and feel for the next step down." I'm sure glad I didn't try this. But about three or four of our party somehow got down to Hoot Owl Ruins and enjoyed the grand view of the canyon below and the distant La Plata Range. They did not hear any owls hooting, however.

Once all of us were reassembled, we hiked northeasterly into a big burnt area. During the summer of 2000, a lightning strike caused a forest fire that burnt 28,000 acres in both the reservation and Mesa Verde National Park. The fire, as harmful as it was, did reveal more Anasazi sites that had never before been seen. We could still smell the burnt and charred wood some ten years later as we proceeded to the edge of a side canyon that the fire had skipped. Marshall led the way through very thick undergrowth of a pine-juniper forest until we almost stumbled upon another set of ruins called Bone Owl Ruins made of thick slabs of bright red sandstone that formed grain storage rooms (for corn grown on the mesa top) and living quarters. These people lived and worked up here back in the early 1100s and left almost two hundred years later during a twelve-year drought. The Southern Utes named this ruin Bone Owl because, when they discovered it, they came across a complete skeleton of an owl in the middle of the ruins. Once again Marshall stood up to wave his arm toward the downward trail.

As he placed his shotgun over his shoulder, we put on our day packs and hopped down the trail until we all came to a sudden stop. Marshall had encountered a very large rattler sunning itself in the middle of the trail. Our guide broke off a dead pine branch and brushed the snake to the side. He kept sweeping the downward trail for a good mile as though sweeping for mines in a war zone. I began to feel like a foot soldier on patrol in Afghanistan seeing Marshall brushing our trail and shouldering a rifle. At last our side canyon entered the much broader Soda Canyon and, as we all gazed upward, we could clearly see a large group of ant-sized tourists at the Balcony House of Mesa Verde National Park. If, by chance, any of them had binoculars that focused in on us, they must have thought that we had become horribly lost at the base of a hot and dusty Soda Canyon.

Though we had a long haul from Soda Canyon back to Mancos Canyon and our cars, we still had plenty of water and lots of time to chat with our friends and to reflect on our day's hike on the rims above canyons at the Ute Mountain Reservation.

3

DESCENT INTO THE GRAND CANYON

LOCATING A CAMPSITE in the dark forest of the North Rim, I quickly set up camp for a few nights and rushed over, with the eagerness of a twenty-two-year-old, to peer into the vast chasm of the Grand Canyon, even if it was dark. The appearance of the moon, just over the rim, enabled me to sense a vast and silent openness before me even though I could not see anything. But I certainly could smell the very rock and cliff of this abyss. By chance, I caught sight of a tiny flickering campfire thousands of feet below me. It was then that I began to sense the magnitude of the Grand Canyon of the Colorado.

Back at the campsite, I crawled into my sleeping bag under the beaming Milky Way and tried to get some shut-eye before my long descent into the canyon along the North Kaibab Trail. I didn't think I got much sleep; however, the pink hue of dawn arrived in what seemed like minutes. I arose in the chilly air of a Canadian-zone forest and soon had my Coleman stove hissing with a bright blue flame that sizzled a pan full of bacon and eggs. With a last gulp of instant coffee and my lunch packed, I made sure my two canteens were filled with icy-cold water. As I trotted over to the trail, I could see distant reds and whites of rock through the evergreen forest. Brushing past dewy ferns, I paused a moment at the edge of the rim to gaze with wonder at this ten-mile-wide and two-hundred-and-fifty-mile-long Grand Canyon carved over millennia by the Colorado River and its many tributaries tumbling from side canyons. And they are all still carving deeper. I could see far across the way the distant snowy San Francisco Peaks, so sacred to the Hopi people of northern Arizona, because these mountains contained kachina spirits who create rain.

I was half tempted to abandon my hike down into the canyon and simply remain up on the rim to stare out at the changing colors of the pinnacles and ravines as the day progressed. But no, I was too young a man to sit and stare all day long as though I were some old Hindu mystic. I just had to experience the depths of the canyon and the challenge of the descent. Besides, the view from far below, looking back up, must certainly be otherworldly. Though I had no Virgil as my guide amid a dense and dark wood, I began my descent into an underworld of geologic infinity. The cool North Rim forest with its Kaibab squirrels, deer, and mountain lions became my past, and the ever-descending trail my present, and the shimmering gray-green Vishnu depths, my future. The upper forest temperature remained a pleasant, if not chilly, forty degrees, but as I dropped lower, spruce trees metamorphosed into yellow desert pines and the temperature rose while ravens squawked. Towering white cliffs rose above me like petrified clouds, and gradually their presence decreased in significance compared to the alluring, dizzy depths below. My orange trail zigzagged below me deeper and deeper until it disappeared as a mirage. There were no longer dewy ferns at trailside, but instead orange-flowered pincushion cactus and scattered, white-flowered prickly poppies.

Lower still and there was no sign whatsoever of Canadian conifers, but instead gnarled, stark, and almost naked cottonwoods. A graceful golden eagle swooped overhead and glided lower into shimmering heat. Now I began to feel layers of heat rising up from the Colorado River basin. Descending lower, I looked back up at the white sandstone heights 2,000 feet above. Was I some kind of sea urchin slithering in the depths of a prehistoric and transparent sea? Snapping out of my desert trance, down, down I hopped like an Apache doing the Mountain Spirits Dance. Sharp-pointed yucca with black seeds in white pods prodded my dream world with desert reality. I gulped down canteen water as though I had an unlimited supply. No, I thought to myself, I need to sip, not gulp! Boy, that water tasted good. I finally caught sight of the pump house some 3,000 feet below the rim and increased the speed of my hopping until, at last, I reached this small building to refill my canteens with treasured water. But when I looked at the pump house thermometer, I could not believe my eyes: 125 degrees Fahrenheit! Three thousand feet could make that much difference in temperature? A sign indicated that Ribbon Falls was but a quarter mile away around a bend in the cliff. Since I had become quite hungry, this would prove to be a perfect spot for lunch. Did the world of the rim still exist? Those aged gray-green canyon walls seemed to answer, no!

The very pleasing white torrent of Ribbon Falls slaked my thirst by just looking at them. I drank and washed my face and began to devour salty, sardine sandwiches. Why on earth would I pack such a sandwich? But, they sure tasted good, and I did have the common sense to pack a peach, a big juicy peach. As I swallowed the juicy peach, thunder boomed as clouds covered the pinnacles above creating in me a strong sense of claustrophobia. No sooner had clouds formed, than a bright sun emerged. I got up to trot even deeper along the trail perhaps a thousand feet lower to a spot where I could at last see just a bit of the chocolate-brown Colorado River far in a dreamy distance. The rocks around me seemed as hot as those on the planet Mercury. But, as Everett Ruess mentions in his letters—at nighttime, "rocks breathe back to the air their stored-up heat of the day." Thunderheads redeveloped in the heat of the day, and thunder boomed and boomed echoing off canyon walls; I half expected to see a T. rex appear from some secretive side canyon. Now the lightning strikes were getting close; I had no other choice, thankfully, but to go no farther and turn around among four-foot-tall prickly cactus bedecked with yellow flowers. I knew that I was in for mountain climbing in reverse. What would have been a descent was now an ascent some 5,000 feet back up to the rim. But I had Ribbon Falls and the pump house ahead of me. The thunder had become more distant when

I reached cool and misty Ribbon Falls. I had to refill one canteen I drained empty between the river view and the falls. By the time I reached the pump house I felt a bit weak and dehydrated. I quickly filled up my canteens once again and proceeded ever so slowly up, up the trail. Within a mile beyond the pump station, I had burnt up a whole canteen of water! Sip, don't gulp! It's one thing to hop down the canyon and quite another to trudge back out, all in one day. Slowly I climbed higher as lightning forked in the distance. Then I saw a mule team perhaps a half mile ahead. Maybe I could catch up with them and get a swallow of water or two. Every time I stopped to sip my dwindling supply of water, the mule team kept moving ahead gradually, distancing itself from me. I had about a thousand vertical feet to go when I ran out of water.

Now that I was out of water, those beckoning conifers way above remained just that—beckoning. I had become weary and dehydrated. It was all I could do to walk thirty feet and rest for five minutes. Then, what do you know, it started to drizzle and soon the drizzle changed to small hail pellets. Lightning jabbed through the skies as I gathered ice pellets to eat. The kachina spirits had taken mercy on me as I quickly regained my twenty-two-year-old strength that brought me back to the cool North Rim with its dewy ferns and resinous smells. By the time I reached my campsite in the evening darkness, I lost all sense of time and space. It seemed as though I had journeyed to some other planet. I thought of that campfire I spotted last night deep down in the canyon and realized that I should have turned this day hike into an overnighter. But now, I wasn't even hungry as I watched a crescent moon set westward beyond the canyon. I grabbed a piece of paper and jotted down a poem:

> Through spruce branches
> at the North Rim,
> a quarter moon set to the west,
> casting shadows from spire to
> spire turning the Grand Canyon
> into the very moon itself.

4

AN ALLURING, ICY LONGS PEAK

Longs Peak, to climb it,
requires a bit of a risk,
but, oh what a view!
—Richard F. Fleck

DURING MY SECOND SEASON as a park ranger naturalist in Rocky Mountain Park and just after my descent into the Grand Canyon, three fellow rangers (Bob Barbee, Dick DeLong, and Jim Jewell) and I planned a midnight climb of Longs Peak at 14, 256 feet, the highest peak in the Front Range of the Colorado Rockies. Bob lent me a paperback copy of Isabella Bird's *A Lady's Life in the Rocky Mountains* (first published in 1879) to read as mental preparation for our climb. There could be no better place to read this book at nighttime than my cabin in the sky at Milner Pass just over two miles above sea level overlooking an Engelmann spruce forest glowing in moonlight. Bird prepared me well by opening my mind and spirit to the mystical glories of 14,000 feet, my first of many such peaks. Her description in the aforementioned book of the lower valleys and distant mountain views is both poetic and painterly:

From this we ascended into the purple gloom of great forests which clothe the skirts of the mountains up to a height of about 11,000 feet, and from these chill and solitary depths we had glimpses of golden atmosphere and rose-lit summits, not of the land very far off, but of the land nearer now in all its grandeur, gaining in sublimity by nearness— glimpses, too, through a broken vista of purple gorges, of illimitable plains lying idealized in late summer, their baked, brown expanse trans- figured into the likeness of a sunset sea rilling infinitely in a wave of misty gold.

Higher up, her climb turned into something different—she was tugged nearly all the way from the 12,000-foot Boulder Field to the summit by a one-eyed man named Mountain Jim. She writes:

The intense dryness of the day and the rarefaction of the air, at a height of nearly 15,000 feet, made respiration painful. There is always water on the peak, but it was frozen hard as rock, and the sucking of ice and snow increases thirst. We all suffered severely from want of water, and the gasping for breath made our mouths and tongues so dry that articulation was difficult, and the speech of all unnatural.

How strange it must have been for Isabella Bird, a Victorian lady, to be standing atop lumpy, frozen ground so far removed from the lush green gardens of England.

I could not wait to climb this peak named after Major Stephen H. Long, who conducted an exploratory expedition to the Rocky Mountains in 1820. He is credited with the first written description of this block-shaped mountain. The Utes (now in Ute Mountain Reservation) may have been the first to climb this peak to set eagle traps on the summit. Why eagle traps? They would pluck war-feathers from these trapped creatures that would then be set free. Major John

Wesley Powell and company are credited with the first recorded ascent of this peak back in 1868, ten years before Isabella Bird.

Our turn came for Longs Peak. Stars shone with absolute brilliance as I drove across Trail Ridge Road to meet my fellow rangers. We signed in at the register at 10 o'clock P.M. to begin a spectacular nighttime ascent of the peak the Arapaho Indians call *Nestoaieux* or "two guides" that includes both Longs and Mount Meeker. Our plan was to arrive at the Boulder Field by midnight, the cables above 13,000 feet by 3 A.M., and the summit itself just before sunrise. We would experience two heavenly phenomena that night, the northern lights and the total eclipse of a full moon. The latter we expected but not the former.

Plodding along the trail above Longs Peak campground, we wound our way through lodgepole pines toward the summit eight miles distant. At first our breathing seemed heavy, and the quiet night air accentuated our human sounds of tramping feet. As our lungs gradually accustomed themselves to the task, we commenced a four-way conversation that had the uncanny effect of disrupting natural silence. Our voices sounded quite out of place in the calm alpine air. Soon we ceased talking and kept our thoughts to ourselves. Only when we stopped to rest did we realize how frigid the air of late July had become. In such chilly air, the very sound of an ice cold brook tumbling over dark rocks made me shiver. Four miles deeper into the forest, we paused by an iridescent stream to fill our canteens and put on some warmer clothing from our packs. Stars peppered the black dome above us. It felt good to be part of a community of climbers rather than a solitary one as in the Grand Canyon a few months earlier. We proceeded onward with a golden full moon rising through creaking branches of spruce and fir. John Muir once described such creaking as a kind of forest violin. We now hoofed along just 500 vertical feet below tree line in a dwarf forest.

The trail leveled out a bit, allowing us to proceed at an easier pace until we reached the Boulder Field at 12,600 feet. This is where the walk ends and the climb begins, as Isabella Bird discovered. The moon illuminated numerous scrubby evergreens growing here and there under the icy masses of Mount Meeker (13,911 feet) and Longs Peak. Gnarled, twisted limber pines, crinkly monument plants, and dwarf willows looked extraterrestrial. At the upper end of the Boulder Field, we all caught sight of the fairy-blinking array of the city lights of Denver some 7,000 feet lower. We stood amid the true alpine tundra zone, with its delicate mosses and flowers barely visible in the black shadows of the mountains. At that time, we did not know about the Boulder Field resting upon a glacier. Only recently, in the late 1990s, scientists discovered that this entire field of boulders spreading over ten acres rests on a six-foot-thick layer of black ice that moves, inches per year, causing the boulders to shift in position. For this reason, it has been determined that there is another glacier (or glacierette) in Rocky Mountain National Park, namely the Boulder Field Glacier, which is in addition to the Taylor, Tyndall, Andrews, and Rowe Glaciers.

Slithering over loose and slowly shifting rocks, we inched our way up Longs Peak flanked by horizontal strips of luminescent white snow. As we rested on a huge boulder, we nervously chatted about the upcoming event—the total eclipse of the full moon, our only sufficient source of light. The eclipse would occur around 3 A.M. and we knew it would take longer than two hours to complete our ascent. We hoped to get past the tricky hundred yards or so of cable (no longer in existence) that aid climbers over a very sheer part of the north face. On went our gloves, as we plodded toward Chasm View, some 13,200 feet high. At this altitude, breathing can be a bit of a problem; our sleepless minds became drowsy and our feet didn't seem to function properly. It seemed as if sheer desire rather than physical prowess pushed us on toward Chasm View.

We all had slight headaches when we sat down on the overhanging ledges at Chasm View. We stared in wonderment at the awesome heights of the famed Diamond Face looming above and at the black waters of Chasm Lake 2,000 feet below. Surely such a place manifests what John Muir meant by the spiritual magnetism of mountains. Despite weariness of body, the spirit seems to ramble out into the cosmos of granite, stars, and moon.

We remained in a trance as Dick DeLong suffered at bit from vertigo; I suppose we all did just a bit. Jim Jewell suggested we climb on toward the summit. Just as we were about to arrive at the point where the cable begins, the moon slowly disappeared. Now, only the stars glimmered above a dark frame of cold rock. Suddenly I shouted, "Look to the north!" Way up toward the Wyoming line, pulsing low in the sky, threads of northern lights began to shimmer as though we stood on some glacier north of Reykjavik, Iceland; it seemed strange that we had to look down at them through crags and notches of dark cliff. Were we on the moon itself? Is that why it disappeared?

We missed the cable. In spite of searching for what seemed like an eternity of minutes in pitch blackness (save for the dim glimmer of our flashlights), we failed to find our iron guide. Worming our way up a narrow chimney in the cliff, we struggled to reach a ledge for a rest. Lo and behold, the cable! The four of us unfortunately had taken the most difficult route to the beginning of the cables, shining so dimly in the granite overhead. Each of us grabbed the cable, took steps, and pulled upward, sluggishly repeating the process many times, like brutes in slow motion. Reaching the top of the cable, we crossed over some slippery, ice-crusted rocks at a snail's pace that tired us to our limits. The moon slowly reappeared. Oh, for a warm sleeping bag to curl up in and doze for a half century.

Attaining an altitude of about 14,000 feet, we had to rest just one more time before gaining the summit itself. The town lights in the warm July prairie far below seemed unreal. A rosy finch flicked past our heads to draw us out of our trance. Bob Barbee shouted, "Two hundred feet to go!" Up we stood, forcing our weary bones to move, until we rambled out onto the small peneplain-summit of Longs Peak. It wasn't difficult to imagine Isabella Bird gasping for breath and being comforted by Mountain Jim.

Since neither food nor drink appealed to us so much as sleep, we stretched out on flat boulders. But only fifteen minutes passed before the chattering of our own teeth awakened us. By this time, while we ate Swedish meatball sandwiches, a faint reddish hue became visible in the frosty air. The dull-green, lake-studded prairie gradually assumed a more realistic appearance. As the sun bobbed up over the rim of the Earth, we all squinted like blind bats at midday. The whole Front Range, all the way down to Pikes Peak, glowed in a golden light, while the narrow valleys far below remained dim and gray. We felt like Ute warriors standing there, arms folded, staring out at the space of snowfield and mountain in the crisp morning air. The distant Never Summer Range glowed in the rising sun; my mind drifted back to the previous summer when I watched a Never Summer flock of bighorn ewes taking turns guarding their lambs. Up here on the summit of Longs Peak something began to happen—the Brocken spectre (to which John Muir refers in *The Mountains of California).* The vast, block-shaped shadow of Longs Peak spread and stretched at the speed of Earth's rotation westward for some sixty miles. We stood in absolute silence. Only once more in my life up to now would I witness such a phenomenon—on top of Mount Fuji, Japan.

Our descent to the Boulder Field proved rewarding. Each foot of granite appeared as varied as would Pennsylvania Dutch farm country from the air—a patchwork of vegetation designs. Orange, yellow, black, and green crusty lichens with dense patches of Irish-green moss and brownish-black liverwort encrusted the cliff sides all the way down to Chasm View. The charm of this color scheme compensated the tired pain of our legs and feet and gave us something to muse on all the way down to the comfort of the valleys below.

I remember years later pointing up to Longs Peak for my Japanese colleague and friend, Minoru Fujita, as we stood on the shoreline of Lake Estes. He said, "Now I understand why you talked so much about the Rocky Mountains when you were teaching at Osaka University!" Longs Peak commands your respect when you look up at it from the valleys below or from Trail Ridge Road where it dominates all of the rolling mountainscapes.

For that reason alone, I had to climb Longs Peak in daytime two more times, once with a fellow ranger and another time, years later, with friends from Laramie just to see if I still could.

With my fellow ranger Mel Lawson, I wished to climb in one day both Longs Peak and Mount Meeker. We arose early on a crisp morning in early July a year after my midnight climb and soon found ourselves walking up the trail above Longs Peak campground. We delighted in the fragrance of the dense lodgepole pine forest. Canada jays squawked and magpies fluttered from branch to branch. A roaring stream tumbled out of Chasm Lake, still several thousand feet above.

Raisins and water replenished our youthful energy until we reached the Boulder Field at the base of a sheer granite wall rising skyward. I gazed across the valleys to Flattop Mountain rising above Tyndall Glacier. Last summer a group of us crossed Flattop, taking the seventeen-mile trek up over the tundra to Grand Lake. In the west-side forests, we gathered fresh grouseberries to take down to Grand Lake where we provided a soda jerk in an ice cream shop a bag full of these berries. He made us, for the first time ever, grouseberry sundaes.

But now we faced the Boulder Field. We slowly trudged up to Chasm View to peer down at an iceberg-riddled Chasm Lake. I had to inch back a bit, as I felt dizzy looking straight down 2,000 feet. Mel and I carefully climbed the cables to cross, ever so gingerly, loose scree up to the summit of Longs Peak; we were far less weary than I and other rangers were during our night-time ascent.

Seeing thunderheads build up to the west, we immediately descended the south face via the Keplinger Couloir and angled toward Mount Meeker. Thinking that we had descended far enough to cross on over to Mount Meeker, we soon discovered that we hadn't gone down far enough to avoid the "Notch," where 200 feet of open space separated the two peaks *(Nestoaieux)*. We didn't dare proceed any farther, as we inched along a very sheer drop-off. Thankfully, we made it back to the summit of Longs Peak! This time we elected to descend, not via the cable, but rather the Keyhole route on the back side of the peak. We followed the painted circles on the rock that guided us down through the chutes and chimneys to the western side of the peak that sported jagged spires touching the sky. One of these spires had a hole in it! We passed through the Keyhole and climbed down to the familiar Boulder Field. All along the trail back to the campground, Mel and I discussed Major John Wesley Powell's ascent with five other men back in 1868. Amazingly, they came to the peak by way of Grand Lake seventeen miles away. Nothing like adding seventeen miles to your climb!

Just a few years ago I had the pleasure of giving an account of Major Powell's climb to an audience at the John Wesley Powell Museum in Page, Arizona. My account was based on my own experience and a close reading of Donald Worster's fine book, *A River Running West: The Life of John Wesley Powell* (Oxford, 2001) in which he provides, in geographic detail, the route from Grand Lake to the summit. Here follows my version.

Major John Wesley Powell and his men regrouped along the shores of deep and blue Grand Lake at the headwaters of the Grand River (after 1949 known as the Colorado River) on a very fine day of August 20, 1868. Powell had been fortunate enough to obtain modest support for an exploring party along the headwaters of the Grand River by the United States Congress, which appropriated monies for rations, and by Illinois college students, who agreed to pay their expense monies to come along and collect specimens for museums back home. During the next summer in 1869, ten of them would explore, with white cedar boats, the length of the Colorado River from Green River, Wyoming, to the Grand Wash on the western side of Arizona's Grand Canyon. Happily, his men, including his brother Walter, Lewis Keplinger, Samuel Garman, William Byers (of *The Rocky Mountain News),* and two local boys, Jack Sumner and Ned Farrell, agreed to climb Longs Peak. The mountain was a great symbol of the beginning of the Grand River, which flowed into the Green River in Utah to become the mighty Colorado River, which in turn, carved its way to the Sea of Cortez (Gulf of California). What a journey it takes from over 14,000 feet down to sea level in 1,500 miles! Certainly they must have had a tremendous campfire the night before their climb. Their campfire reflected off the waters of Grand Lake as sparks danced skyward to meet the stars. The sky with the Big Dipper, Jupiter, and Mars held their attention beyond sleeping hours. There was the faintest trace of a shimmering, faint-green aurora borealis. Powell hardly noticed the pain in the stump of an arm, amputated after the Battle of Shiloh only a few years before.

A hearty breakfast of fresh trout and fire-roasted potatoes more than prepared them for their first day's hike, as they followed the North Inlet through a dense lodgepole pine forest. At a higher elevation, spruce and fir sweetly perfumed the air. Their packs contained rations for more than a week. Their pack mules toted bacon, flour, water, a Dutch oven, bedrolls, and some scientific equipment. Much to Powell's pleasure, Keplinger, an eager college lad, led the way.

It is not difficult to imagine that they must have observed such things of nature as a small and delicate nest with tiny beaks protruding skyward, awaiting a mother hummingbird who buzzed her wings just beyond reach of their beaks. They would have marveled at the mother as she pushed her beak into their wide-open mouths to give each of them a dose of mountain nectar. Such clear, azure blue skies they had never seen before. The American West is great, thought Major Powell, for more than its wealth of minerals! Each breath of air restored a wholeness to body and spirit.

Their way grew steeper and the air much thinner. Up there the trees appeared stunted and twisted by winter winds, yet these possessed a sublimity of their own. Garman, their Quaker companion, reflected on the peacefulness of the scene. If only humans could live in such peace, he remarked. Having suffered the wounds in the War between the States, how could Major Powell not agree? They paused to take a drink of icy stream water, so cold it made their teeth hurt. They all took out some hardtack and jerky to make a light lunch for themselves as they listened to the splash of waterfalls tumbling down from mountain snow. They rested on rocks coated with orange lichen and fleshy liverwort. Indians said that a person could survive on liverwort if no other food was available.

A crashing and crackling of rocks sliding off some broken ledge above startled all of them, including their pack mules with bulging eyes. The rocks fell through space, as if in slow motion, thumping harmlessly into an alpine marsh lush with glacier lilies. They all stood in a trance, but soon Powell advised his men to push onward and upward. Ideally, they should camp above tree line along a lake's shoreline, if possible, where they could catch trout for dinner and breakfast by means of hand lines. Just as they emerged from the forest, a giant bull elk came running through the valley, crashing into young trees and knocking them over. Was a mountain lion in pursuit? They could only guess.

One can imagine Major Powell's words: "Let's climb a little higher. Let's find a nice lake above tree line and build a campfire there. I want each of you to carry as many broken branches as possible for firewood."

After some tramping, they spied a small lake that the men later named in the major's honor. It lay beneath the steep tundra slopes of a high peak glazed with bands of cold mist. They selected a camping spot, dumped their collected firewood into a nice pile, and soon had a roaring fire. The two Powell brothers and the Quaker walked over to the lake to fish with hand lines baited with baby grasshoppers collected the day before in a lower, grassy valley. After an hour or so in the dying rays of sun, all three of them had nibbles on their lines and, at last, yanked in five or six fingerlings each. They ambled back to camp, proud of their strings of fish.

"So, what was it like fighting in the Civil War, Major and Captain Powell?" asked the Quaker student.

"I'd rather not talk about it at all," said Powell's brother, Walter.

"We fulfilled our obligation," said the major very quietly, "and while it was extremely frightening and terrible with men suffering and dying all around, it's something that had to be done. But I agree with my brother, let's not talk about it, especially under these magnificent clear skies of Colorado!"

Powell tried to protect his poor brother from the devastating memories that caused him such mental anguish. The major offered Walter a pipe filled with tobacco fresh out of his pouch to calm and soothe him. "Yes, will you look at those stars, Walter." When he at last puffed on the pipe and sang a little tune to himself, Powell walked over to Garman and asked him why would he ask such a foolish question, especially coming from a peace-loving Quaker.

"I didn't mean it that way. I meant to draw out of you two some of your heroic deeds, but I see now that I made a mistake. I'm very sorry."

After dinner, a cool breeze chilled them to the bone. They all went over to the rope-shackled mules to get bedrolls for some sound sleep before a steep ascent to the tundra the next morning.

A glorious sunrise shone into their faces, awakening them out of their slumber. The mules chomped on lush grasses as the major prepared a fire from the previous night's embers, put on coffee, and baked some sourdough biscuits in a Dutch oven carried in by the pack animals. With a tin mug of coffee in hand, he examined the steep slope they had in store after breakfast. He spotted several bighorn sheep silhouetted by the sun in the high tundra. A marsh hawk sailed overhead in pursuit of small field mice, no doubt. The men all seemed eager to climb up into the sky and gain their first view of Longs Peak. Rather than taking the pack animals any higher, Powell suggested to his men to build a corral of fallen logs in the forests directly below the lake.

Shortly after securing the mules, they shouldered their packs loaded with bedrolls, hardtack biscuits, and water. The major even placed a small bottle of wine in one of his pack's compartments. William Byers remarked that he had never seen such steep terrain as he, and others, huffed and puffed their way through soft grasses and entwining dwarf willows. Thistle plants turned their heads toward the early morning sun. Pikas and marmots peeped and squeaked in the still air. They could barely see over a western ridge into the vast expanse of Grand Lake and the distant, snow-laced Gore Range. They all marveled at the delicate, penny-sized alpine forget-me-nots carpeting the tundra at their feet, and at the bright golden sunflowers bobbing in alpine breezes. And then, as they angled toward the top of the ridgeline, all they could see was a huge dome of sky. They stood, within minutes, atop an unnamed peak, looking across a vast abyss of space to McHenry's Peak and a distant, molar-shaped Longs Peak darkening in summer storm clouds. Powell's men embarrassed him by naming the peak upon which they stood "Powell Peak." Why not leave them unnamed, or find out what their Indian names are, he thought.

Jagged lightning bolts forked the eastern skies about twenty miles away. Moments later, thunder boomed and rumbled and boomed again in this thin alpine air. Illinois thunder sounded nothing like this primal, prehistoric thunder. They sat in a circle and ate some biscuits topped with bacon slabs and heartily drank water from their canteens. A marmot came begging for food, but they were all too hungry to share any of it with him.

"Well, lads, see yonder peak—McHenry's—let's follow the contour of the terrain over to it and see if we can get across to Longs Peak," but Ned Farrell wanted to linger a bit more just to soak up all this beauty.

They put on their packs, strapped on their canteens, and trekked across incredibly soft and spongy tundra. They clipped along at a fast pace, and within forty-five minutes stood atop McHenry's Peak. From there they could see across the valley filled with moraines all the way to the Mummy Range and the distant high plains of Laramie with its recently completed Union Pacific Railway. Within a year this transcontinental railway would be connected at Point Promontory, Utah. Major Powell would then be able to have cedar boats shipped to Green River, Wyoming, where his great exploratory expedition of the Colorado River would begin in 1869.

"Hey, my friends," shouted Jack Sumner, "there appears to be a narrow ridge of rock connecting our peak with Longs. Look slightly downward and eastward!"

"Right you are," said the major.

They immediately hopped down to the narrow, somewhat frightening ridge, and picked their way slowly and carefully across it, trying not to look down 2,000 feet on either side, as the ridge was only a foot and a half wide in places. Distant thunder rumbled as a storm slid harmlessly eastward. Powell's companions used both arms to balance themselves in the wind—a difficult task for the major, who had only one arm. Wind gusts became dangerous. Major Powell feared that one of them might slip. Only very slowly did they approach Chief's Head Peak, sticking up in the sky. Suddenly, Jack Sumner froze with shaken nerves; he couldn't move an inch farther. Keplinger carefully edged past him. He then encouraged Sumner to continue onward with success. Longs Peak remained dream-like and far way. Reaching the summit of Chief's Head, they realized their mistake. There was nothing but gaping space across to Longs Peak. Small pipits flicked past their heads, paying no heed to the depths below.

"I have an idea," said the major. "Let's get ourselves back to McHenry's and descend into the basin below. Look at all those nice lakes! Yes, let's descend with care and set up camp on the south side of Longs Peak, then try to climb it from there. Apparently there's no way of getting over to its west-facing or north-facing cliffs."

"I agree," said Keplinger. "Perhaps there is an accessible route up the south side."

The six men proceeded ever so slowly down the flank of McHenry's into this southern basin (now called Wild Basin) and breathed sighs of relief when their feet touched flower-clad tundra instead of loose, wobbly rocks. Powell sat down or rather fell down, in the soft tundra grass near a pile of August snow and admired yellow, springtime buttercups growing right out of the snow. Here is where the summer season is crowded out by springtime blossoms and approaching autumn snows. Is there really a summer in the tundra? As they tramped lower toward tree line, they brushed past pink elephant-heads and marsh marigolds growing along icy rivulets. Warm bands of valley air rose to greet them after their chilly alpine scramble off McHenry's Peak.

Angling down toward a lake with deep snowbanks, William Byers twisted his ankle on a protruding root. Thankfully, after they bound it with cloth, he was able to walk, very gingerly, along the shoreline. It proved to be only a slight sprain. They rested a bit before descending even farther to a sandy-shored lake that was within a direct line of Longs Peak's southern flanks. Here they would camp for the night before attempting to summit Longs Peak, rising some 3,000 feet above. Powell felt at home by this sunny lake with its thin stand of timber and subalpine fields of purple monkshood and bright blue *Mertensia*, or harebells. They set up camp only several miles east as the crow flies of their previous night's camp spot—just a rocky ridge of McHenry's Peak separated them from their pack mules. The evening before their final ascent became quite chilly, making it difficult to fish with numb fingers, but fish they did and with success—four large cutthroat trout. Just before darkness, they feasted on fire-roasted trout, sourdough biscuits, and fresh-perked coffee, topped off with a surprise from Keplinger—a tin of juicy peaches from the depths of his pack. The Milky Way, or as the Indians said, "The Way of Souls," spread across the inner dome of heaven. The sweet scent of a resinous pine branch fire made them sleepy in the warmth and comfort of their bedrolls. But another rock slide awakened them late in the evening. It seemed to have come from the upper flanks of Longs Peak and fell into the soft tundra above them. The major hoped this event would not prove to be some sort of omen.

At the slightest hint of daybreak, they awakened one by one. Sumner built up a breakfast fire and put on the coffee. Each of them, huddled around the fire, stuck a wooden stick into a thick slab of bacon and cooked it to crispness. Eating done, they prepared themselves for an exploratory climb to the base of the peak via a delightful small alpine lake that they named in Keplinger's honor because he led the way across yesterday's knife-edge ridge. Little rivulets of melting snow trickled into this lake, feeding the roots of marsh marigolds as golden as the rising sun. A stream tumbled out of the south end of Lake Keplinger, making a pleasant gurgling sound in an otherwise silent alpine amphitheater. Noticing something bobbing in and out of the outlet stream, Powell walked down a steep hill fifty vertical feet. To his delight and surprise, the bobbing motion proved to be that of a water ouzel, or dipper bird, in search of underwater prey.

"Major, what are you doing down there? It's up we want to go!" shouted Keplinger.

"A water ouzel caught my eye," was the major's response.

Keplinger, proud of his knife-edge bravery, proposed that he lead the way up, because he thought he saw a perfect route up the south face—a sort of narrow couloir. The rest of them slowly followed his lead, but some of them, including Powell himself, began to feel the effects of prolonged high altitude, or perhaps the bacon hadn't properly settled in his stomach. Keplinger climbed so fast that he finally completely disappeared from view. The major worried about his decision. What if he ran into trouble five hundred feet above? However, not being able to do much else, he and his men trudged ever so carefully higher and higher until they stood on a ledge affording them a view of Chief's Head directly across a dizzy abyss. Orange and gray lichen coated almost every rock. Green and gleaming mosses dripped with icy water. Powell looked above to see Keplinger coming back down the cliff.

"Major," he shouted, "it's far too steep and scary up there!"

"How close were you to the summit?"

"I'm not sure, but maybe within 800 feet."

"Well, Keplinger, I suggest we all get up to that very point in the couloir, and surely all of our sets of eyes will spot a more encouraging route up the last bit of cliff."

"I need to rest, Major Powell, I feel a little shaky."

When he returned back down to their level, they all sat in comfortable positions on a ledge to the left of the couloir. It had become midmorning and already they heard very distant rumbles of thunder. Yet the sky above was cobalt blue. A raven high above, floated on thermal layers of air and let out a deep, raucous squawk. Hawks, higher up, perhaps redtails, circled to the east over Mount Meeker. Perhaps they had spotted a dead animal of some sort.

"Are you rested, Mr. Keplinger?"

"I suppose so, Major Powell."

"Then let's go."

They climbed a couloir slowly but steadily as they looked down on the distant Indian Peaks to the south. The couloir narrowed down to a mere chute. This very location proved to be Keplinger's high point.

"Let's proceed up the chute using our shoulders for friction," Powell suggested.

"But Major Powell, what if the chute peters out with nothing but over-hang?" asked Keplinger.

"We'll deal with that when we get there!"

Except for scraping his stump ever so slightly, causing a toothache-like pain, the major managed to negotiate the chute well. Others behind him kept on plodding upward as though heaven itself were their destination. More thunder, this time a little closer. Powell could not help but notice a dark patch of cloud to the west. Keplinger, who had eased ahead of the major, disappeared from view. What is that man doing? Powell disappeared from view and so did three others including Walter, leaving Byers alone on the side of the cliff. Why had they all disappeared, Byers thought to himself. They stood on the summit, that's why! And then all six of them stood in the sky standing on a small pene-plain covered with dark slabs of frozen rock. A chilly breeze, too chilly for their thin garb, numbed them to the bone. Powell carefully removed a barom-eter from his pack and took a measurement. There they stood on August 23, 1868, on the summit of Longs Peak at 14,256 feet above the level of the sea and some 6,000 feet above Grand Lake and the winding Grand River. The view? Unbelievable! Kansas stretched eastward. A vast array of the Rocky Mountain chain loomed to the north. They could discern the faint but very white Medicine Bow Mountains of southern Wyoming. Major Powell's cedar boats would travel by rail in just nine months around these mountains to Green River City. To their south, they could see very clearly Pikes Peak and all the rugged mountains in-between. To their west, they looked, with smiles, at Chief's Head, McHenry's and Powell Peak, and the more distant Never Summer

Range. Beyond this range, they could see the great Colorado Plateau stretching on toward Utah. They felt like Ute warriors up there on the roof of the American West so high above the Grand River. Immediately below them lay the sublimely picturesque valley of Estes Park with its shining glacially polished knobs and dense forests. Powell's spirit soared like a hawk.

"Well, don't just stand there and stare, you fellas," said Keplinger. "Sign your names on this sheet of paper! When you're finished, I'll put the document inside this old baking soda tin and place it under a rock so men of the future will know that this is the first recorded ascent of the great sentinel of the plains—Longs Peak!"

Mr. Byers, though quite weary, took out his notepad and pencil and jotted down some thoughts for a *Rocky Mountain News* article. Then Major Powell brought out his surprise bottle of wine and christened their baking soda tin mountain register. He offered all a sip, except for Garman, who shunned such extravagance and even warned Byers not to include his name as one who indulged in wine. They all stared at each other, wondering if it all wasn't a dream. Powell was so proud of his men. They could have easily refused to make this arduous climb by lingering along the pleasant shores of Grand Lake so far below. Thunder boomed, this time even closer, and they made a careful but quick descent down the narrow chute to what became known henceforth as the Keplinger Couloir.

Approaching the lower end of the couloir, the major felt just a bit dizzy, but happiness overruled. Pipits flicked past their heads as they hopped down to the bottom of the wider couloir, and within an hour or so they trekked across the tundra toward that ridge that separated them from their pack mules. Keplinger and Garman wanted to take further measurement atop McHenry's Peak. Powell told them to watch for sudden storms. The rest of them took the much easier route across soft green tundra, down to Lake Powell and their corralled mules. They caught and roasted cutthroat trout that peeled right off the bone and into their mouths.

"Well, my lads, what do you think of yourselves now that you've climbed to the highest point above the Grand River?"

"We're almost too tired to think at all."

"Into your bedrolls, men, and sleep well."

"I hope Keplinger and Garman are safe up there by McHenry's Peak," said Sumner.

"Oh, they'll be quite all right. We'll see them in a day or two back at Grand Lake," said the major.

He couldn't sleep at all until, perhaps, the wee hours of the morning. He kept thinking about that view atop Longs Peak. He couldn't bear waiting nine months to get into their white cedar boats that were being built in Chicago. The major could see in his mind's eye Green River City, Wyoming, far out in the rolling sagebrush desert. He could even hear the piercing train whistle as it pushed away from them toward Utah, while they shoved off a small island in the stream to begin their river run into the great unknown.

5

STEEP TRAILS IN ROCKY MOUNTAIN NATIONAL PARK

I—Specimen Mountain

THE YEAR BEFORE climbing Longs Peak at night, I remember leading my first group of people on a wilderness hike up 12,482-foot Specimen Mountain on the west side of the park. This extinct volcano, seen clearly from Fall River Pass and whose crater was gashed open by ancient glaciers, is studded with a spruce-fir forest below its tree line at 11,500 feet. Because its opened crater is full of salts, bighorn sheep gather here to treat themselves to a giant salt lick. Its high, bald summit is challenge enough for a leisurely day's hike up a steep trail. Specimen Mountain has been extinct for over 10,000 years, though the park's earliest naturalist, Enos Mills, claimed that nineteenth-century Utes (Marshall's great grandparents) of the area had legends of the mountain's puffing smoke.

I met my group at 10 A.M. at Poudre Lake on the Continental Divide at 10,000 feet. Fifteen people varied in age from ten to seventy and in profession from businessmen to college professors. One man had returned just six years earlier from the Korean War and remarked how similar this national park is to the mountainous terrain of north-central Korea. Thirty years after my ranger days,

I had the occasion to visit South Korea whose landscapes did indeed resemble the alpine zone of Rocky Mountain National Park, but not because Korea has alpine tundra but rather its rugged hills remain bald from American fire bombing.

We started up the trail through a lush subalpine meadow coated with rosy and red Indian paintbrushes, white pearly everlasting, and bright yellow marsh marigolds. There was a slight chill in the air, but our hiking steadily upward kept us warm. Just as my group was getting broken in and walking at a steady pace, a 150-pound black bear suddenly appeared within forty yards of us. A Chicago businessman excused himself and returned to his car even though the bear lumbered up into the woods away from us. Fourteen remaining people seemed all the more determined to move on and experience all they could. The ten-year-old child in the group picked up a beautiful arrow point, chocolate brown in color with perfect symmetry. Since the Ute Indians hunted this area a century ago, my best guess was that the arrow point belonged to an ancient Ute hunter.

When we reached an altitude of around 11,500 feet, I pointed to dwarf spruce trees, no larger than a thumb, growing in dense mats close to the ground. If a botanist were to do a tree ring count, he would have to use a magnifying glass, so compressed and tiny are the rings. Such a tree as this could have over one hundred rings proving that these dwarf trees can be over a hundred years old. Arriving on the high green tundra, the Korean War veteran had to leave and return to his car. In his own mind, these similar landscapes brought him right back to Korea and machine gun fire. Unfortunately he missed seeing a large snowfield fringed with bright yellow snow buttercups growing right up through the shallower edges of snow. As we paused to take pictures, a white-crowned sparrow serenaded us with his notes: *ah-tee-tee-tee.*

The remaining thirteen people and I developed an esprit de corps as all of us started to feel a oneness with this high tundra of the Colorado Rockies. A hoary marmot or whistle pig greeted us with his high-pitched squeaks at the saddle some 11,700 feet above sea level. It is important to note as I write this, that as of the turn of the twenty-first century, hikers must stop at this point since this area is now a protected habitat for bighorn sheep. But back in 1959 the trail continued to the summit of Specimen Mountain. My group took a rest at the saddle and enjoyed the tremendous view of the vast Never Summer Range or *Ni-Cheebe-Chii* in Arapaho, literally meaning Never-No-Summer. They rise as the park's western-most ridge above the valley of the Colorado River that begins, as a mere trickling stream, in Rocky Mountain National Park (founded in 1915) at Thunder Pass. Directly below us lay ashes and vents of the glacier-gashed crater where bighorn sheep fed on scrubby grasses and licked the volcanic salts.

Since those good old thunderheads began to build up, I suggested pushing on to the summit of Specimen Mountain. The trail sharpened steeply, but all members of the party kept chugging along. Some of us began to breathe quite deeply in the thin air above 12,000 feet. My weekly hikes up Specimen Mountain would certainly prepare me for Longs Peak. After we stopped for a rest and some water, one spry lady in her early seventies set the pace for my whole group. Because I became winded trying to point out this feature and that, I finally remained silent for the last 300 vertical feet. The volcano's features became more and more distinct the higher we climbed until we stood at last on the summit at 12,482 feet (around the same elevation as the Boulder Field). While we ate our brown-bag lunches, we could see for a hundred miles northward and southward from the Gore Range of Colorado to the Snowy Range of Wyoming. The sky darkened as we finished our lunches and swilled some coffee. We had no other choice but to descend quickly. I had grown to like these people even though they were perfect strangers only hours ago. It was difficult to say good-bye back at Poudre Lake where it had already begun to rain and sleet.

II—Mount Chapin in Winter

After my seasonal ranger job had ended, I began my graduate studies at Colorado State University but could not resist joining the university outing club. During the Thanksgiving holiday, we returned to Rocky Mountain National Park to make a winter ascent of Mount Chapin, a tad lower than Specimen Mountain. But what a difference deep snow and ice makes!

We all boarded my old jalopy and several other cars to drive across red sandstone hogbacks covered with damp, gray-green sagebrush. We wound our way from Fort Collins by back roads toward Big Thompson Canyon. Five of us would climb the mountain while the rest prepared a Thanksgiving dinner at a friend's cabin. Rolling mile-high prairie spread below us, purple with haze and dotted with bright lakes and ponds gleaming in the sun. Aged and leafless cottonwoods fingered their way across the sunny prairie. We entered a dark canyon with granite cliffs rising hundreds of feet to meet the sun, creating a haiku of contrast. By now, any inner stagnation of mind had dissipated. Jack pines clung here and there on the layered canyon walls, scenting the air. The roar of the cascades of the Big Thompson River intensified as the river rounded the Pillar of Hercules, a sheer eighty-foot rock face rising out of tumbling white water and marking the entrance to Big Thompson Canyon. All we could think of was making a winter ascent of 12,454-foot Mount Chapin, the first of the Mummy Range.

We turned off the Big Thompson road onto Devil's Gulch Canyon road, where scaly-barked Douglas fir and red-barked ponderosa pine swayed and creaked with late autumn breezes. As we continually gained elevation, the balmy, late Indian summer air of the prairie gave way to the chilling winds that raced down from the high country. In a somewhat protected hollow, a few aspen trees, still with withered leaves, trembled. Twisting our way up the dusty switchbacks, we became aware of how stark the aspens, willows, and cottonwoods had become. We at last gained a view of the broad, open valley of Estes Park, glistening with sparkling fresh snow. The whole Mummy Range spread before us, including Mounts Chapin, Chiquita, Epsilon, Fairchild, Hagues, and commanding Mummy Mountain (13,425 feet). What a perfect day for our climb, thought we.

Driving past scores of mule deer, elk, and several coyotes scampering through Horseshoe Park, we continued our last motorized lap up several hairpin turns on the old Fall River Road, some thirty-five years after my grandparents had driven a Model T Ford all the way from Philadelphia past walls of snow leading up to Fall River Pass. They wrote across the top of their photos,

"Summer Snow!" We put on our packs and winter parkas at Chasm Falls, anticipating a fair share of winter snow.

Our ten feet commenced a slow but steady pace over crackling, dead bracken ferns and through dense stands of lodgepole pines. We hoped to reach the shoulder of a ridge that led to tree line at the base of Mount Chapin. The extreme steepness of the trail and the weight of our winter gear tired us quickly, since we were not yet acclimated to this 10,000-foot elevation. Climbing over logs, dried Canada thistle, and crusty patches of snow, we continually gained altitude, noting that lodgepole pines had yielded to thick stands of incredibly tall Engelmann spruce and subalpine fir. We, at last, arrived at a windswept shoulder of Mount Chapin where the temperature dropped by twenty degrees. The whole panorama of the terrain through which we had traveled spread before us. The wind, however, made it quite difficult for us to maintain a hold on hard-packed ice.

After a mile or so of plodding through foot-deep snow, we found a rocky promontory where we warmed up with hot soup, bread, and coffee. The usual Canada jays hopped around, begging for food. Their squawking attracted smaller but hardy winter residents—gray and black chickadees. This brief rest with food gave us the energy necessary to forge on toward the summit. The comforting squeak of chickaree squirrels gradually faded as we entered the tree-line zone at 11,500 feet. Squat and twisted limber pines hissed in the ever-howling wind. It had become cold enough to make us shiver if we did not keep moving. There was no bare ground—just frozen, icy snow. Blasting gusts of acid-stinging wind howled above matted groves of dwarfed spruce, warning us of what was to come. No longer would we have the shelter of a warm forest. The temperature hovered around zero, with screaming wind sounding somewhat like the South Col of Everest. Breathing became difficult at 12,000 feet, and I felt such a fatigue as I had never experienced during my summertime climbs.

But our weariness soon abated. There, as we edged our way around a stony knoll, six bighorn rams walked calmly and gracefully on frozen alpine terrain as though they were taking a stroll in Central Park in May. As we stared at these creatures, storm clouds began to gather. We moved on toward the summit across treacherous ice. The sheep, however, obviously thought slippery ice was mere child's play. They continued to amble along, unconcerned with us or an approaching severe storm. Our summit loomed above us by only several hundred feet, but the ice harassed us every inch of the way. Climbing fifty feet or so, we arrived at the base of a hard-packed snowfield encrusting the mountain's crest as far as we could see. Out came our ice axes, and slowly we began carving steps up the steep, white slope.

When I reached the halfway point, I stopped to rest and look out into the heart of high country. My sense of novelty at being in such a precarious position in a howling wind quickly changed to trepidation. Like a starfish, I clung tightly and slithered my way up until I reached the summit. Oh, for some summer desert heat! Up here the wind proved powerful enough to flatten me. All five of us stood hypnotized by sheer vastness of space. To the south lay the ice-blanketed Mosquito Range, framed in the foreground with block-shaped Longs Peak, weathering the wind like a ship at sea. To the east, clear to Kansas, stretched the Great Plains in crystalline air. To the west and north, we saw more rugged and storm-smothered mountains of western Colorado and southern Wyoming. In, fact the thin and rushing air up here remained momentarily so clear that a myopic person could dispense with his glasses.

Soon, however, quickly advancing storm clouds swept in like a desert dust storm blurring our vision. "Let's get the heck out of here," I said, hoping all my friends could hear me. They must have, because we descended as quickly but as carefully as we could. But icy boulders forced us to stay on mental alert every second of the way like skiers going down a double black diamond trail. By the time we made it to the upper reaches of tree line, big flakes of snow sprinkled down on us like confetti. At last, we heard the friendly chirping of chickadees from the lower spruce woods, and then we heard the roar of Chasm Falls, not yet frozen. Already it grew warmer and warmer as we descended through the snowy woods. In the lower lodgepole pine forest we actually removed our sweaters. We arrived by sundown at the cabin and were greeted by those who had prepared a Thanksgiving dinner. A roaring log fire comforted us as we sat down to the tastiest turkey dinner of our lives, made all the more memorable with sage and pine-nut flavored stuffing. What a pleasure it was to eat pumpkin pie and drink hot coffee without a single worry of frozen boulders, icy wind, and approaching storms from the west.

III—Mummies in Summer

My third season as a ranger came with duties at information desks and guiding short nature walks. I did manage to get in some cross-country hiking from Fall River Pass over to Comanche Peak where I heard, in the distance, the roar of a mountain lion. But it wasn't till August that a group of us hiked up steep trails to the highest peaks of the Mummy Range well over 13,000 feet. From 8,000-foot Horseshoe Park, the hiker can clearly see the mummy-like configuration of this mountain range by tilting the head sideways. All six of the Mummies stand in view with Hagues Peak rising the highest to 13,560 feet. We selected Hagues for this day's challenge and looked forward to getting a bird's-eye view of Rowe Glacier, the only glacier in the park above 13,000 feet.

We began our slow trek up the Lawn Lake Trail with our backpacks and canteens rattling in unison. In a matter of minutes, we gained altitude rapidly as our trail switched back and forth, giving us a broad view of flat-topped Deer Mountain. We rambled through peaceful groves of lodgepole mixed with aspen, following the Roaring Fork River that tumbled down from 11,000-foot Lawn Lake. Here a dam had been built before the national park was established in 1915 to serve the purpose of water diversion for dry-land farming in the prairies below. Just twenty years after our climb of Hagues Peak, this dam burst after a week of steady torrential rains in 1982. A wall of water roared down the canyon taking with it trees and boxcar-sized boulders that tumbled into Endo Valley, sounding like the end of the world. I would read about this in the *Mainichi Daily News* in Japan where we lived for one year, the year we climbed Mount Fuji. Canada jays screeched along our trail just beneath the jagged and glacially carved west face of Mummy Mountain (13,412 feet). Lower forests now gave way to dense, aromatic stands of Engelmann spruce and silvery, sappy subalpine fir. From here, amid scrubby evergreens growing as mere bushes with bare roots clutching the soil, we gained a superb view of Hagues Peak way above us and, at last, the glistening waters of Lawn Lake. In contrast to rocky, alpine heights, soft and delicate yellow marsh marigolds gleamed in the wetlands nestled beneath jagged cliffs that rose above the bluest of blue lakes.

A shoreline ranger patrol cabin lay just ahead of us with a fireplace, some bunks, and a dirt floor. An icy spring gushed from the rocks just outside the cabin. We rested our weary bones after taking a drink of ice-cold spring water. Trout rose in the middle of the lake, tempting us to linger here all day long. But we methodically pushed on toward higher ground, following a steep trail beyond the shorelines of the lake, and in no time we trekked above tree line. At one spot on the trail a little beyond tree line, we gained a superb view straight down 500 feet to Crystal Lake at the foot of Mount Fairchild. We took the saddle approach to Hagues Peak at 12,400 feet and thence up the cliffs for the next 1,100 feet. The snow-blanketed Never Summer Range constantly caught our eye. But stubborn Hagues Peak still rose above.

I came down with a sharp headache but continued to climb right up to the base of the peak where I began to feel a bit dizzy. The only other time I ever had altitude sickness was high in the Wind River Mountains of Wyoming. In deference to me, we stopped for a rest on a flat, boulder field some 13,200 feet high where I sipped hot tea before having a bite to eat. Tart-tasting lemonade along with a beef sandwich helped restore my strength and spirits. I had no difficulty whatsoever springing up the final bit of cliff to the summit. From atop Hagues Peak, the pure white and wrinkled surface of Rowe Glacier hypnotized us. It nearly covered (in 1961) a modest-sized lake that is the source of the Big Thompson River. Rowe Glacier (formerly Hallett Glacier) was discovered in 1876 by the Hallett Expedition when it was twice as large as it was in the 1960s. But Rowe appeared to us to be large enough being about a quarter mile long and 100 feet thick. Pale green pan ice floated peacefully on the lake. Because this ice body is slowly moving over its own pressurized and "plasticized" interior, it is called a glacier; otherwise it would be merely a static snowfield.

Staring at Rowe Glacier brought me back to my day on the rugged surface of Paradise Glacier hugging the flanks of Mount Rainier, where I followed the banks of a clear, cold stream until it completely disappeared under ice. There I rested a wee bit while enjoying a glacial symphony. Rivulets trickled and dripped like the abstract expressionistic music of Arnold Schoenberg. My mother, sitting on an ox-horn stool at my father's Parnassus Bookshop in Princeton, said that she hated the icy-cold music of Schoenberg. But had she heard these irregular-sounding glacial drippings, who knows what she would think. Schoenberg himself was Austrian. Had he been inspired by the sound of these drippings? Rocks constantly tumbled off the lava ridges of Rainier, sometimes rolling to within a few yards of where I stood daydreaming. I hiked a bit farther across the snow until I spotted an open patch of river flowing underneath. Gingerly, I crawled deep into the hole some ten feet below to be within the white roof of a giant's mouth. Hunching over, I took a couple hundred steps into a bluish-white ice cave until I could no longer see the sky. Sitting down on an exposed rock fifteen feet under the base of Paradise Glacier, all sorts of thoughts whirled through my head. Even though I was as removed from humanity as I possibly could be, in here I felt a very strong sense of kinship. It was as though the stones in the stream were given eyes, and the icy water itself were given ears, and the lumpy layers of ice—a heart. My humanity became its voice, and its "mountaineity" became my mode of expression. If only for a few moments in the ice cave, I began to "think like a mountain," to use Aldo Leopold's words. When I emerged, Mount Rainier looked brighter than ever just as it can look sometimes for the people out in the Puget Sound.

We gazed to the north beyond Rowe Glacier to see the Rawah Range and the upland prairies of southern Wyoming. On the horizon, through our binoculars, we could actually discern tiny dots of buildings in Laramie, Wyoming, some sixty air miles distant. Little did I realize that I would be living in one of those tiny dots for some twenty-five years, teaching at the University of Wyoming.

Since it was still only early afternoon and no thunderheads threatened us, we decided to return via the summit of Mummy Mountain. The descent of the cliff proved to be relatively easy until we reached the top of a mile-long boulder field. Did it, too, possess a dark glacier underneath like the one on Longs Peak? Each and every boulder we stepped on wriggled and rocked, and after about thirty minutes of continually catching our balance, we sat down exhausted between Hagues and Mummy. Perhaps a vast network of black, quasi-underground glaciers that gradually move caused all this wobbly, rocky instability. As I stood up, I instantly spotted a dead Clark's nutcracker, a large, jay-sized bird with gray, black, and white coloration. It was most surprising to see a dead one in that they are supposedly very strong fliers and rarely crash-land. I imagine, though, the wind currents and downdrafts at this altitude can be quite treacherous to man and bird alike.

I felt every inch of the way going up the slopes of Mummy Mountain from the boulder slabs. Fortunately, we walked along the gentle eastern slope of the mountain. Mummy Mountain, like most of the Colorado Rockies, has one side carved-out by the glaciers of the Wisconsin Ice Age some 10,000 years ago. During this period the ice advanced and retreated up to four times. It is this carved-out side that is exposed to Lawn Lake. The other side is a gently rolling peneplain. Before long, we stood at the rock cairn marking the summit. Longs Peak rose across the way with its surrounding court of Chief's Head, McHenry's Peak, and to the east Mount Meeker.

Soon we bounced down the terraced slopes of the south flank and gradually descended into the stunted trees of the krummholz (tree line) area. Not being on a trail, we had a bit of difficulty keeping our bearings once we entered into a dense forest. The Lawn Lake Trail had to be directly below us, but how far below we did not know. Naturally, when one thinks he is close to home at the end of a journey, he really is not, and such was our case. In order to get to our trail, we had to ford three streams, climb down two steep cliffs, and crawl through a briar patch. All this reminded me of my frantic state when I got lost on Mount Ida a few years earlier. I had to descend, during a violent thunderstorm, to an unfamiliar lake (the wrong lake) where no friends awaited me with coffee and sandwiches. Instead, being at an unnamed lake, I had to trample through trailless forests downhill to the Colorado River Valley for some eighteen hours before entering civilization. But now, thankfully, we reached the Lawn Lake Trail. Our legs felt like pounded steel and our stomachs growled like timber wolves. With each thud of our mechanical feet on the homebound trail, we felt more and more like stiff Egyptian mummies. Perhaps the person who named these mountains was not thinking about their configuration alone.

6

HIGH, WIDE, AND WINDY: THE PRAIRIES OF LARAMIE

"Prairie" is a French word meaning meadow or grassland, but it's far more than that. First of all the Wyoming prairies are a land of scant rainfall. The prairies of Laramie receive only nine inches of rain per year which classifies them as being "semidesert." These prairies are full of ravines sometimes brim full of choke-cherries ready for the picking by early autumn. They are home for sage hens, jackrabbits, antelope, prairie dogs, badgers, western meadowlarks, and coyotes. Nothing is more refreshing and nostalgic than the sound of coyotes yelping at a prairie moon rising above a remote western town. And nothing scents the air quite so pungently as sage, especially damp sage after a fresh springtime rain. If one has a bit of luck, he may find rings of stone in a fifteen-foot diameter called "tipi rings" marking ancient campsites of the Arapaho or Cheyenne Indians.

I know of no better place to acquaint oneself with the high prairie than Laramie, Wyoming, up on a high hump of the planetary rim over 7,000 feet in altitude. Walk one mile out of Laramie and you're on it, and it stretches for hundreds of miles beyond. The prairie skirts up to the beginning of the snow-glazed Rocky Mountains (including distant Hagues Peak) with a carpet of flowers, sagebrush, rabbitbrush, yucca, and grasses. It is no exaggertion to say that on the prairie, land is drowned with sky, a big sky. Just walk along nineteenth-century Overland Trail and you'll be convinced of it. There are many lakes on the Laramie prairies hollowed out by the wind as John McPhee explains in his geo-poetic book *Rising From the Plains*. Another body of water, a twisting one, is the Laramie River. I remember looking down at the prairies from a twin-engine Cessna. The most striking thing about that brown autumnal prairie is the curving Laramie River looking like a human capillary furnishing the skin of the earth with nutriment.

Winter comes early to the Wyoming prairies with winds that would put the South Col of Mount Everest to shame. I remember as if it were only yesterday skiing cross-country with my son past an ancient cottonwood tree onto the frozen, windy prairie in a late afternoon sun. Rich and I skied down icy ravines and step-laddered up opposite sides to glide across flat stretches and take off our skis on exposed, stony slopes, and put them back on to ski down even steeper, icier ravines. It was like being on some Himalayan expedition; the wind howled like a maniac, drifting hardened snow around tufts of sagebrush stretching onward toward an infinity of lunarscapes. We took refuge in the shelter of an old cowshed. To the far west rose the Snowies with constant mystic bands of snow banners waving outward like prayer flags at a Buddhist temple halfway around the world in the Himalayas. Boards from the cowshed lay scattered about, becoming all the more gnarled and bleached by a strong sun in the thin air, one and a half miles above sea level.

To the immediate east rises the Laramie Range, once called the Wyoming Black Hills. Dark, pine-fringed canyons snake their way down, looking like spiritual entrances to our Earth Mother. From high up on an even windier plateau of this range, one can readily see across the clear prairie to the Snowies of southern Wyoming and the Rawahs of northern Colorado. Here is where prairie meets mountain (the very meaning of the Arapaho word *Wyoming*), a gangplank of sorts raised over sixty million years by the Laramide orogeny according to John McPhee. And this gangplank rises from the eastern Great Plains.

From all directions comes power for the human spirit. Nicholas Black Elk, holy man of the Ogalala Sioux believed (knew) that the North brought a spiritually cleansing wind, and the South brought growth, fertility, and warmth. The East brought birth, peace, and illumination, while the West brought storm and conflict and even death. By sitting out here in early winter, you can sense all of this, especially by facing south and the glowing warmth of the sun. But surely strong, "cleansing" winds can come howling in from the North. My son and I were thankful for the cowshed as the wind became even fiercer. In the distance, Earth Mother rose eastward with her dark and sheltered canyons filled with frail aspen and dried chokecherries.

Northward stretched an immense open and snowy space much like the view we experienced of looking northward in Þingvellir National Park up in Iceland where snowy and glaciated mountains loomed ever northward. Vast bands of whitened land spread onward to meet the pale blue of winter sky. Winds swept across the rippled waves of snow from the northwest, dropping the chill factor to something beyond human endurance. To the south, more gray clouds concealed the blue-gray planetary humps of thickly forested foothills barely revealing the distant frozen mass of Hagues Peak. It was time to return home to a crackling fire and the warmth of my wife's laughter during a cold and stark winter when we all looked forward to the coming of spring.

Spring does come by slow degrees to the prairie, sometimes far too slowly for those of us with cabin fever. As the snow melts leaving thin windows of ice here and there, sagebrush tips underneath the clear ice panes begin to green. And if it should rain, helping to produce that annual amount of nine inches, in late April, the sagebrush will scent the entire prairie surrounding Laramie with pungency. When one smells sagebrush and hears coyotes yelping, he knows it's got to be spring. But hold your horses! At 7,200 feet snow can fall on the greening prairie as late as the end of June just when zucchini squash blossoms are blooming in the backyard. It is then that the prairie most resembles tundra. Between the melting snow patches, tiny flowers including white sandworts and purple pasqueflowers start to bloom. Rosy finches, pipits, and western meadowlarks cheep, chirp, and warble under the bluest of skies. And, if one is lucky, he'll see the colonies of yucca in full bloom with stalks of creamy blossoms that will turn into "Navajo bananas," or prickly pear cactus bedecked with waxy yellow roses. It doesn't take long to spot a herd of antelope running faster than race dogs and leaving clouds of dust behind. And when the dust settles, behold a prairie dog standing up on its hind legs scouting the terrain. He's lucky; he doesn't have to worry about rattlesnakes because the elevation is too high and the soil too alkaline (these prairies were once an ancient seabed). Biologists consider this environment to be an extension of southern Canada—a little piece of Alberta 700 miles south. In fact, a species of toad usually found in Canada thrives here near Laramie—the Laramie Plains toad. He is considered to be a residual creature stemming back to the last Ice Age.

I threw another stick on the fire that crackled and sparked under prairie stars of early summer. My daughters and I camped on a high, wooded rim overlooking Laramie. I told them that once the entire prairie below was full of bison; they used to migrate up to the high prairie from the lower eastern plains (that extend back to Illinois) over the gangplank of the Laramie Range for summer grazing. The Plains Indians in ancient times raced the bison herd over the edge of *pishkuns,* or buffalo jumps, and finished them off with arrows. They believed that this creature was a true gift from Wakan Tanka or the Great Spirit, as it fed and clothed them and furnished them with bone tools, utensils (soup ladles made from the hip bones), and ceremonial implements. Four and seven are sacred numbers for the plains tribes, and four times seven is the most sacred of numbers: twenty-eight, and twenty-eight days are in the lunar month and twenty-eight ribs has the bison, one rib for each lunar day. Imagine what the prairie looked and sounded like! One town in Wyoming got its name—Chugwater—from the sound bison make when fording a stream. Lewis and Clark once watched an immense herd cross a tributary of the mighty Missouri River. It took nearly three hours for this herd to cross. Now, as Buffy Sainte-Marie sings, "Where have all the buffalo gone?"

"Where have they gone, Daddy?" asked Maureen.

I put another stick on the fire and told her that soldiers and professional hunters like Buffalo Bill killed them by the thousands and heaped them up in rows out there on the prairie a hundred years ago in order to starve the Indian.

"Why?" asked Michelle.

"Because we wanted their land. But things are more hopeful now. We're beginning to appreciate tribal cultures more and the buffalo are coming back from the few animals that remained in the late nineteenth century. Yellowstone National Park and Custer State Park (South Dakota) are homes for thousands of them. Some northern tribes in Montana now have small herds of them. There's a professor at Rutgers, Fred Popper, who has suggested that a portion of the arid Great Plains be reverted to a "buffalo commons.""

"That's good," Maureen said.

"Well, girls, we'd better get some shut-eye. Sleep tight."

Two owls hooted in a lonesome grove of jack pines not far away. The moon rose through them like dim recollections of the past surfacing to consciousness. I got up to put a few more sticks on the fire to watch the sparks rise up to the stars. By a Montana campfire years ago, the poet Vachel Lindsay told the essayist Stephen Graham that sparks do not die. "They only seem to die; they go on, like ideas, into the invisible world." He wished to write an adventure of twelve sparks, he said to Mr. Graham. I dozed off under the Big Dipper until a chorus of robins, sparrows, and meadowlarks awakened me at dawn's faintest glimmer.

Henry David Thoreau concludes Walden with these words: "Only that day dawns to which we are awake. There is more day to dawn. The sun is but a morning star." Never before had those words meant so much to me as on that prairie rim at daybreak. To witness the coming of dawn, I climbed a rocky upcropping where I could see nothing but dark prairie and a dim outline of the distant Snowy Range. Then, ever so gradually, like a plate of sensitive film, the Snowies appeared white, then rose-colored, and then radiant gold. As the sun rose, the band of gold spread downward from the mountaintop to foothills and prairie and Laramie itself. Truly there is more day to dawn, most especially a prairie dawn.

7

WHERE LAND
IS MOSTLY SKY

I—Grays and Torreys

HOW CLEAR IT WAS that morning when three of us unloaded our gear from the car to climb two 14,000-foot peaks in central Colorado near Loveland Pass. It had been reported that the summit of Grays Peak experienced a short but furious burst of popcorn snow the day before. We all felt a little apprehensive about climbing two peaks the same day. I hadn't climbed a fourteener since my thirty-fifth birthday twenty years earlier when I climbed Longs Peak for the third time. Now I was living in Denver, as were my two companions. Although we were all in our fifties, we remained, nonetheless, eager to climb two peaks in the high tundra where land is mostly sky. The jagged glacial ridge leading up to Grays and Torreys Peaks jumped out at us in the clear air. It had an extra-terrestrial look—all rock with just the slightest suggestion of green vegetation gleaming in the rising sun.

Down along our trail grew dense groves of willows, whose yellowing leaves gently rustled in the morning breeze. Ravens circled high above, following the contour of the surrounding glacial cirques. Father George Schroeder led and Mark Reames and I followed, sometimes stopping to admire Colorado columbines and sometimes craning my head to look at billowing clouds that took on shapes of the mountains underneath. George disappeared around the bend. By the time we reached him, he was on his knees in the subalpine grasses, not praying, but photographing a whole field of sun-glinted flowers that included yellow and rosy paintbrushes, bright-blue harebells, purple penstemon, and white bistort. "Vincent Van Gogh would have gone wild here," I remarked and George answered with a grin.

By now, subalpine willows grew as mere mats huddled down low as much as possible out of the constant wind. We noticed some white dots above. Were they mountain goats or just rocks? At last they moved. We continued trekking along the trail and stopped frequently to catch our breath, as we were now well above 12,000 feet. People above us stood still, looking intently at something. Huffing and puffing, we arrived at their level on the mountain to see a female mountain goat in a shaggy coat with her three kid goats all staring directly at us. Jagged peaks came into view to the north and east along with several other fourteeners, including Mount Bierstadt and Mount Evans and Longs Peak to the far north. We could also make out several high thirteeners like Arapaho Peak and Square Top. One year earlier, Mark Reames and I had sauntered up to 13,400-foot Arapaho Peak, with its jagged summit looming over the wrinkled mass of Arapaho Glacier, the water source for the city of Boulder. Mark recalled that this glacier had receded considerably since the early 1940s. Soon we could not see anything to the south and west save the high, looming slopes of Grays directly above and Torreys to our right. We had to climb still higher to cast an eye on the Collegiate Range with Mounts Princeton, Harvard, and Yale.

The soil under our feet appeared sparse and stony. A few tufts of alpine forget-me-nots coated the immediate foreground. From such a perch it was easy to agree with John Muir that the mountaineer climbs mountains with more than feet or hands:

In like manner the soul sets forth at times upon rambles of its own. Our bodies, though meanwhile out of sight and forgotten, blend into the rest of nature, blind to the boundaries of individuals. But it is after both body and soul of a mountaineer have worked hard, engaged hard, that they are most palpably separate. Our weary limbs, lying at rest on the pine needles, make no attempt to follow after or sympathize with the nimble spirit, that apparently glad of the opportunity, wanders along down gorges, along beetling cliffs, or away among the peaks and glaciers of the farthest landscapes, or into realms the eye had not seen, nor ear heard; when at length we are ready to return home to our flesh-bone tabernacle, we scarcely for a moment or two know in what direction to seek for it.

But *our* bodies reminded us that they were thirsty and hungry. The summit looked insurmountable. It seemed to rise higher and higher. We now stood above 13,000 feet, and it had become chilly, but not so chilly as to make us put on parkas. In the bracing air, we slowly edged a bit higher to walk out onto a promontory ridge where we caught whiffs of fresh forest air from lower depths. Longs Peak looked close enough to hit it with a stone.

More mountain goats gathered on rocky ledges below us. Their beards fluttered in the steady breezes. Alpine flowers, looking like miniature fiery suns, bobbed on their stalks, and tailless pikas squeaked in high pitch, punctuated our alpine flow of thoughts. I could discern tiny human figures apparently standing on the top of Grays Peak, recalling my ascent of Mount Fuji in which droves of Japanese pilgrims hung over the edge of the volcanic peak to shout words of encouragement to climbers lower down. Mark Reames, who had lived in Japan for more than twenty years, read my thoughts, saying, "No teahouse here to refresh us!" Seeing a marmot scurry along the trail gave us incentive to keep pace, slow though it was. We arrived at the point where there was nothing but sky all around the rocky ridge just ahead. That ridge eventually yielded until we stood on top in a little circle of rocks surrounded by a universe of endless mountain ranges.

The Mount of the Holy Cross rose to the far southwest, as well as scores of other peaks of the Saguache Range, including distant Shavano and Antero. And to the extreme southwest, we just barely discerned the hazy Maroon Bells and heavily glaciated Snowmass Peak. Like Buddhist monks high in the Himalayas, we turned slowly in circles, absorbing the cosmos, until a sudden shower of popcorn snow caught us by surprise and coated our hair as white as mountain goats. We smiled. All this reminded Mark of his experiences in the Japanese Alps, which are inhabited by white snow monkeys. He loved to watch them scramble and play in fresh snow.

Out came our sandwiches and juice. We ate heartily amid an August snowstorm at 14,270 feet atop Colorado's ninth highest peak. During our lunch, several shaggy mountain goats outstared us with their shiny, dark eyes. Far below we could see a little piece of Interstate 70, with its mad scramble of ant-sized cars headed for the Eisenhower Tunnel. Although we could not see the entrance to the tunnel, we could readily observe the buzzing ants' destination—the wide valley of Lake Dillon and several ski areas below a dark puff of cloud that would probably surprise the ants once they got through the tunnel.

Father George, Mark, and I were game to go ahead with our plan to ascend a second fourteener that loomed a half mile west of us. We would have to descend a thousand feet or more to the saddle and then painfully regain the elevation lost. Torreys Peak is only three feet lower than Grays. Of course, the scramble down to the saddle was a cinch, except for a few wobbly rocks. The sun broke through the clouds—a welcome sight as we passed by several crusty snowfields at the saddle and slightly above us. And then, as Torreys' pitch increased, I felt my leg muscles tire—no wonder, after climbing Grays Peak a short while ago. All I could see was rock and sky as we slowly edged toward the summit.

We paused to catch our breath by photographing a sparkling snowfield or a bright yellow cluster of lichen that coated the boulders. Breathing became difficult. Perhaps the combination of Grays and Torreys was beginning to take its toll. I began to doubt my strength. Was I going to make it? Where were George and Mark? Had they vanished into thin air? And then I realized that they stood on the summit just overhead. They weren't miles away after all. A few huffs and puffs and I saw their faces. A few more, and I saw their entire bodies against the sky. They stood among a herd of mountain goats, and Father George was talking to them. "Thank you, gentlemen, for sharing your marvelous home with us!"

After resting five minutes at 14,267 feet and drinking some cold water, we all felt restored and energetic. Several other climbers joined us and engaged us in a discussion about which mountain range was which and which ski area was Breckenridge as opposed to Keystone. Mark, the native Coloradoan, settled these issues with a tone of finality. Before making our descent, we cast one more glance around the universe of alpine terrain that consisted of lower reddish ridges, distant gray peaks, azure-blue skies with cumulus clouds, and the distant mass of Mount Evans and Mount Bierstadt to the east, perhaps twenty-five miles away. We tentatively agreed to climb one more four-teener, probably Mount Bierstadt, after a two-week sojourn in the city of Denver somewhere far below. We waved good-bye to our fellow mountaineers (both humans and goats) and began our rapid descent to the saddle between the peaks.

Halfway down to the saddle, it began to snow, only more furiously than on Grays Peak. The sky had become completely gray and the winds increased. Instead of going all the way down and around the base of Grays, we looked for cutoff trails down the hollow bowl between the peaks. I followed the crest of a snowfield while my two companions took a surer route along the bottom edge of the snow. I told them I would meet them down yonder where the snowfield trail and the talus trail joined, perhaps 800 vertical feet below.

Just a month earlier, I had climbed Saint Mary's Glacier above Idaho Springs to the green tundra. I had stopped and stared at a grazing cow elk some fifty yards distant. When it came time to descend the glacier with its steep pitch, I instinctively traversed from one side to the other instead of going straight down and risking a slip. Today I felt quite comfortable on this snowfield, even though it had a rather steep drop-off to jagged rocks eighty feet lower. Apparently the dizzy angle had frightened away Mark and Father George.

As I traversed the steep snow patch and angled down toward naked rocks, I noticed that George and Mark had only begun their descent into the bowl. The increased wind and snowfall had me worried just a bit, especially when a conversation I had with my neighbor came to mind. She said she slipped and slid upside down on one of those Torreys' snowfields but fortunately arrived head-first harmlessly on grassy tundra. I kept moving with caution until all three of us edged closer to the rendezvous point in a mixture of driving sleet and snow. The going was nasty, and I was glad to be down in the glacial bowl, out of the wind. We were all close enough to talk to each other with our voices echoing off talus slopes. "How's your trail?" I shouted. "Slick as grease," they shouted back. Before long, we no longer needed to shout. My trail descended rapidly over muddy rills and wobbly rocks. Quite a barren place, I thought to myself, as I hadn't noticed so much as one flower.

It was good to rejoin my companions. Grays and Torreys looked like monstrous giants about to hurl lightning bolts at us. Eventually, though, we walked through more grass than rocks, and happily our trail joined the main route off Grays Peak. The sun returned full strength, and we stopped to take off our icy, hooded parkas and gulp down some refreshing water from our canteens. Since we had expended much energy, both psychic and physical, the relatively simple descent proved wearisome. Father George stopped suddenly. We caught up with him and knew why. We listened to the wind in the willows. The sound varied in intensity and pitch with each gust of wind giving a unique voice to the mountain. Ravens sailed above, following wind currents. Willows, wind, and birds soothed our minds and made us forget the pain of our tired feet. We became a set of winged Mercuries descending the last slope with a message of the mountain's glad tidings.

II—Bierstadt

Mount Bierstadt, rising just west of Mount Evans, was named after Geman-born artist Albert Bierstadt (1830–1902). One of the last artists of the Hudson River School of painting, his works are characterized by vast panoramas of the Rocky Mountain West. I remember standing in front of one of his Wagnerian scenes at the Buffalo Bill Center in Cody, Wyoming. A horrendous lightning storm arched itself between two gigantic peaks of the Wind River Mountains of Wyoming. I believed that I could actually hear the wind, taste the rain, and feel the crackle of electricity, even though I stood in a warm museum. Although the vegetation was wrong, and the mountains rose absurdly high, the mood and atmosphere were right. The painting brought me back to my own experience in Yellowstone of climbing Mount Washburn high above Dunraven Pass and looking across at Electric Peak to the northwest where a thunderstorm started to unleash itself. Nowhere else does thunder boom and echo louder than in the Great American West.

Twelve days after our climb of Grays and Torreys, Father George Schroeder and I and two new climbing companions, Willy Sutton and Ike Rodman, met at the little town of Grant, Colorado, at 8 A.M. to drive up to Guanella Pass and climb Mount Bierstadt (14,036 feet). The mountain would live up to its namesake by providing us with a Wagnerian overture.

At Guanella Pass, we were not certain which trail would lead us to Bierstadt's summit. The reason? A half dozen trails meandered into thick groves of willows that dropped from the 11,600-foot pass to 11,000 feet or so in the vale between us and the base of the summit. We decided to bushwhack our way through, sometimes feeling like Humphrey Bogart aboard the *African Queen* in search of the main channel of the Bora River to Lake Victoria. Just when we thought we found a way, the willows thickened up. George, wearing alpine short pants, fell into a hollow and almost disappeared completely. By the time we got to him, he had already managed to pull himself up on his feet laughing all the while. Realizing he was not hurt, we all joined in with laughter.

At the bottom of the vale of willows some five or six hundred feet lower than the pass, we forded a stream, sunk ankle-deep in subalpine marshes, and backtracked several times around incredibly thick clumps of willows. All of this could have been avoided if we had simply gone over to the northern edge of Guanella Pass and picked up the established trail, which even has wooden walkways across marshy areas. Nonetheless, we forged up the willowy base of Bierstadt until we arrived, at last, on relatively free and open tundra at perhaps 12,000 feet. Grays and Torreys had nothing like this. Their approaches seemed relatively simple in comparison. At least the snowfields had not scratched our arms and legs the way the willows did.

Willy and I stopped frequently to photograph flowers and catch our breath. Willy coined a new name for the Russian thistles that covered the mountainside. He called them "eclipse flowers" because they looked like a bunch of miniature dark eclipses with the morning sun behind them. Between the spiny thistles grew bright-red Indian paintbrushes, and down in hollows of rock, a cluster of dwarf columbines helped create a tundra palette with colors enough for the western artist Jacob Alfred Miller or Albert Bierstadt himself. A circular pattern of crusty green lichens, a foot and a half in diameter, smothered the side of a rock and looked quite literally like an artist's palette. Such a growth could easily be 150 years old. It served as a "base camp" for future mosses that, in turn, would harbor dusts and soils. Perhaps a few hundred years from now, tundra flowers and dwarf willows will sprout from this very rock.

Willy tapped me on the shoulder and said to look around. I had been so involved with the tundra before me that I had failed to notice how high we had climbed. To the west, in dark shadows, rose the twin peaks of Grays and Torreys. On the day we climbed them, Torreys looked far more rugged than Grays, but from this distant perspective, we could see the jagged, south-facing side of Grays that clearly matched the rugged north-facing side of Torreys, the face we had been exposed to during our ascent twelve days ago.

To the southwest we could make out the peaks of the Sawatch Range, but our view remained obscured by the ever-rising slope of Bierstadt. Father George and Ike rested on rocks a hundred yards or so beyond us. They looked like two alpine mammals of some sort, so much did they blend into space. Ike and George continually discussed the existence of God, Ike being the doubter. Father George could not have had better props to argue in God's favor than the sublimity of an immense alpine panorama surrounding and dwarfing us all.

After frequent stops to catch our breath and admire close up the "eclipse" thistles with their heads bent downslope and minute cushions of purple phlox, we caught up with Ike and George in the midst of their dialogue at the saddle between a false summit and looming Mount Bierstadt. Here we could finally see the massive, tundra-clad Mount Evans (originally named Rosalie, after Bierstadt's wife) rising to the east and a deep, rocky gorge containing Abyss Lake. The gorge served as an echo chamber for the high-pitched squeaks of tiny, rabbit-like pikas that scampered on lower ledges. We estimated that we stood at about 13,000 feet. Several years later, my wife, Maura, and I, along with our little cocker spaniel, Mini, would scale the West Arm of Mount Evans along frighteningly steep ledges across the way. And Mini and I would climb Bierstadt a year later on a cold and windy Labor Day. At the summit, we would huddle together for warmth behind a windbreak of rocks.

But on this summer day, Willy and I joined George and Ike to push ahead, with the false summit gradually sinking behind us. Thunder rattled. Rock slabs rose above, and I knew then that we had arrived at a point where land is mostly sky. We waved a weary hello to other climbers and walked over to the summit's northern edge. We peered down several thousand feet into a rugged glacial cirque containing Abyss Lake. Thunder boomed all around us, and the skies had darkened dangerously. But the sun shone down on us. Father George said rather whimsically—for Ike's benefit—that if the Red Sea parted for Moses. . . . A mixture of rain and snow zoomed in on us while lightning bolts danced in the skies not too far away. We took some photographs and quickly dashed down the trail to a rocky shelter where we could eat our lunch.

Mount Bierstadt lived up to its name. As we sat huddled between 13,000 and 13,500 feet, torrents of rain with lightning etched the sky to the south, while an equally impressive storm zeroed in on the nearby mountains to the north. Bearing down on us from the west came a third storm. But where we sat, the sun beamed on us as though we had been placed right inside a Bierstadt canvas.

We feasted on a communal lunch. Willy sliced his garden-fresh zucchini squash, which served as bread. I sliced my delicatessen feta cheese. Father George shaved off pieces of spicy salami, and Ike peeled his oranges. Willy served as the assembler of zucchini sandwiches. We ate faster than Willy's hands could move, but he continued to produce satisfying morsels until we had gorged ourselves. There was enough left over to feed several mountaineers. Father George paralleled our 13,000-foot feast—for Ike's benefit—with Christ's multiplication of loaves and fish. The principle of sharing multiplied tenfold the joy of hungry men eating, which, in turn, dissipated fears of inevitable storms.

We got up on our stiff legs and picked up a clearly marked trail that dropped off at an almost dangerous pitch down to the valley of willows. We didn't want to get blasted by lightning and made a very fast descent. Within an hour, we were thrashing our way through willows dampened with rain. I looked up at Bierstadt, covered in mist and cloud. It looked higher than Mount Everest from this willow jungle. I couldn't imagine a better way to have intensified and energized our lives than these few hours above the din of our daily travail.

8

A SCRAMBLE UP
TABEGUACHE

STINGING SLEET CAME in waves from ever-darkening clouds to the west. My boots were wet and my knees were wobbly, yet we had to continue down to safety, having climbed the southernmost peak of Colorado's Saguache Range—Tabeguache Peak. Unconcerned mountain goats grazed peacefully on a grassy ledge a half mile away. Their wet, white wool shone in a beam of sunlight that punctured billows of gray clouds.

Just forty-five minutes ago we stood atop Tabeguache Peak. There we nibbled on crackers and oranges and stared into space. To the north rose Mounts Antero and Princeton, and across the way to our immediate east stood Mount Shavano, gray and bald in an early September sun. We could not see from this vantage point the legendary snowfield in the shape of an angel that lies on Shavano's eastern flank. Legend has it that a young Tabeguache Ute woman prayed for rain during a severe drought and willingly submitted to sacrificing herself toward this goal. Every spring a snowfield appears in the shape of an angel—the angel of Shavano. We continued our gazing southeastward toward the distant and somewhat hazy Sangre de Cristo Mountain Range. A brisk wind buffeted us up there with a temperature in the low forties. We knew that Denver was roasting in the nineties and took some solace in the contrast. More than once we ducked from diving swallows flying precariously close to Tabeguache's summit and our heads. Food and the view energized us. But we worried about a lightning-charged sky with a fast-approaching thunderstorm.

We gingerly proceeded with our lateral descent across scree and loose rocks covered with brilliant lichens that varied in color from orange to green, and emphasized all the more with splats of rain and sleet. Black clouds raced in from the west. It looked grim, but we steadily descended from Tabeguache's lofty 14,157-foot summit to 13,000 feet, recorded on my son's altimeter. Amazingly, the clouds dispersed and the sun poked through as we reached a south-running ridge with camel-like humps. Each step up one of these humps came with cramps in my legs and knees. We saw bighorn sheep to the west moving along ridges with graceful agility. We paused for water and dried Turkish apricots and noticed clusters of alpine sandworts and elk sedges whose sepals already had begun to turn crimson. From wooded valleys far below came the sound of squeaking, rusty castle gates slowly opening and closing—bull elk bugling to signal the beginning of rutting season.

Last night, in our primitive campsite at 10,500 feet, we had been serenaded by elk mystically bugling from both afar and near. In the tent, I had drifted back to my ranger days in Rocky Mountain National Park when I was stationed at Moraine Park. It was autumn and the first heavy, wet snow had fallen. Mist had risen, phantom-like, from the meadows, and hundreds of elk had bugled in rapid succession. It had seemed like I was on another planet. Writing accession numbers on museum specimens did little to dispel the faraway feeling. Another loud elk bugle brought me back to our tent beneath Mount Tabeguache.

I looked out our tent window very early in the morning and thought about the tribe for whom this mountain was named. Shavano was a leader of the Tabeguache Ute tribe and befriended white settlers in these south-central mountains of Colorado. I pictured Shavano looking something like our Ute guide Marshall back at Mesa Verde. I could readily imagine the frustrated look on his face when more and more miners came in search of gold on the very flanks of Tabeguache and Shavano Peaks in violation of the Brunot Treaty of 1873 signed by the Utes. Chief Shavano's trip to Washington, D.C. to protest these intrusions a few years later proved as fruitless as November grouseberry bushes. Eventually, the government forced this mountain tribe to live in the arid southwestern corner of Colorado on the Ute Mountain Tribe Reservation.

Before getting out of my sleeping bag, I remembered planning this trip with maps of the Saguache Range spread out on our table. Tabeguache had stood out at the beginning of this range, flanked by high thirteeners and Mount Shavano. We had chosen to ascend Tabeguache the following Saturday morning in early September.

I recalled that my son Rich, in drowsiness, thought he saw a large, four-legged animal through the tent walls the night before our ascent with one of Rich's friends sound asleep in his own tent. I had remained asleep while he worried whether or not it was a black bear or an elk. Apparently, whatever it was, it wandered away harmlessly, as my son had recollected. We arose early, as did our friend Michael in his tent. We immediately poured coffee and ate breakfast bars as we packed our day-sacks for the climb ahead of us.

The morning remained as clear as the previous starlit evening. We found the trail and bounded straight up through an aspen grove all aglow with golden and orange leaves and soon reached a dead-timber zone. Each twisted and nude trunk looked like the kingdom of Oz. But the steepness of the trail forced us back to reality. That trail was no tourist trail—it went straight up with loose gravel and pebbles. We would take two steps ahead and one sliding step downward. It was tiring—very tiring. The flanks of Mount Shavano, however, gradually came into view, as did high thirteeners to our west and the distant Black Canyon of the Gunnison, the deepest canyon to be so narrow in North America. The tundra of September had a distinct rust color. We at last reached a fairly level tundra plateau and drank water and gobbled trail mix. White spots on the distant tundra proved to be a flock of mountain goats. We put on fleece jackets in a stiff wind. Clearly, autumn had arrived at this altitude. Just two weeks later I would fly over Mounts Tabeguache and Shavano on a flight from Las Vegas to Denver. They appeared out the aircraft window all white under mounds of fresh snow.

Then we arrived back at this very spot on our way down. This time we saw up close two bevies of ptarmigans changing from summer to winter plumage with fluffy white feathers underneath. Despite the approaching storm, my son took a close-up shot with his new camera while Michael and I stared at the birds, their beady eyes staring right back. More clouds rolled in from the west and gusts of wind pelted us. Though my knees were hardly prepared for the straight-down, loose-gravel trail, I had no other choice but to follow, as best as I could, two agile young men who danced down the trail toward the safety of tree line. Cautious at first, I inched my way down but gradually allowed myself the freedom of sliding in the dust. It was, nonetheless, tiring work. Perhaps fifteen or twenty minutes later I arrived where Rich and Michael sat in dead tree branches like eagles awaiting my arrival. It remained chilly even some 2,500 feet lower than the summit.

With wobbly sets of knees we continued our trek down this steep trail to the thicker forests of golden aspen. Rain splattered down, making the trail too slick for any rollicking. Each step was taken with utmost care. I could no longer see my young companions ahead. The trail seemed endless. True, I had gotten past the loose rocks, alpine winds, and sleet pellets, but the trail remained tiresome. I arrived at a little fork in the trail and hoped that I was taking the right one back to the road below. I spotted my son waiting for me at the bottom of the hill, and it felt great to see him. We ambled slowly down the trail and out onto the road, where Michael was changing his boots to more comfortable, softer shoes. We were all thankful to have made this climb, my twenty-fifth of seventeen different 14,000-foot peaks. Tabeguache challenged all three of us, and it pushed me to my physical limits at age sixty-six. How could I not but feel a sense of exhilaration despite temporary weariness? In its own way Tabeguache Peak provided us with something close to a vision quest, showing us throughout our climb our utter dependency on nature as well as our own inner strengths.

9

FOUR-CORNER HIGH

I—Uintas

MY COMPANIONS PREPARED for the Uintas, each in his own way. Mark Reames practiced hiking with his new backpack days before our excursion into eastern Utah. Willy Sutton camped in southern Utah, photographing petroglyphs and pictographs in the Grand Gulch not far from the Perfect Kiva, while I finished teaching a summer class in Rocky Mountain National Park. We all had the Uintas on our minds; there we would climb for twenty-five miles in the only major range of mountains in the Rocky Mountain West that runs east-west and not north-south—the Uinta Range.

The Uintah Utes believe that these mountains are sacred because their base is surrounded by a circle of red sandstone. They believe that when this world comes to a violent geologic end, survivors will assemble within the sacred ring of Uinta sandstone to form a new tribe of what was once Turtle Island, or North America.

The Uintas have a unity all their own. Perhaps they were, according to University of Wyoming geologist Carol Frost, part of a much older plate (up to

3.9 billion years old) around which other plates gathered. This much older plate, made up of the bulk of present-day Wyoming, northern Utah, and eastern Nevada, could have been the original Turtle Island, covered with tropical palm trees, billions of years before humans had arrived. Some tribal people of the Great Plains believe, according to A. C. Ross of Pine Ridge, South Dakota, that humans have been in North America for millions of years but as disembodied spirits. Those ancient spirits became familiar with each and every nook on the mountain ridges of the giant turtle's back.

Why do the Uinta Mountains run for one hundred miles east to west, unlike all other major Rocky Mountains? A good question. It is curious that Split Mountain, Utah, to the east, is swirled, if not twisted, toward the Uintas. Several geologists have speculated about their east-west orientation. Philip B. King in *The Evolution of North America* (1959) believes that they are a Middle Proterozoic sedimentary formation that was originally part of the Siberian-North American rift zone, which was subsequently uplifted more than 13,000 feet. King wrote, "Like the Uinta Mountains themselves, the Uinta Mountain Group (including environs) extends eastward, and it probably accumulated in an aulocogen, or rift in the continental platform like the Precambrian-early Cambrian of the Wichita system in Oklahoma." A later-day geologist, John D. Cooper, in *A Trip Through Time* (1986), agreed with King that the Uintas are part of an aulocogen, or "failed rift," between Siberia and North America, which were east and west of each other. Today, however, Carol Frost has cast some doubt on the rift theory in that this old core plate is from 3.5 to 3.9 billion years old. Lands on both sides of the Pacific are younger, not older. The Rockies, for instance, are infants of only 60 million years. There is still the question of why the Uintas (having quartzite older than 2.5 billion years) run east to west, unlike the Wind Rivers of Wyoming, the Wasatch Mountains of Utah, the Sawatch Range of Colorado, and the Front Range of Colorado. Perhaps they are like Robert Frost's "West-Running Brook":

What does it think it's doing running west
When all the other brooks flow east
To reach the ocean? It must be the brook
Can trust itself to go by contraries.

The Uintas must trust themselves going by contraries, and therein lies their unity of purpose.

Mark and I had to meet Willy in Vernal, Utah, by 6 P.M. We nonetheless stopped for lunch two hours out of Denver on Vail Pass. There we sat in silence, watching strands of clouds gather like modern glaciers filling up hanging valleys of the Front Range. Rosy paintbrushes and purple larkspur scented the fields before us. Distant Torreys Peak, which we had climbed the year before, darkened in a gray and threatening sky.

Mystical mist continued to collect on the rock ledges of Glenwood Canyon and along the volcanic dikes north of Rifle as we journeyed on toward Vernal. We passed through a violent thunderstorm, with hail splatting against our windshield, near Dinosaur National Monument on the Colorado-Utah border, making for one of the wettest deserts I had ever seen or smelled. After a rain, gray sagebrush and juniper and pinyon pines scent the desert air like the most delightfully pungent incenses in a Buddhist temple. Desert air revitalizes the soul. In the desert, the mind is led skyward, to a sky that is robbed of all moisture by the dry terrain below.

The twisting box canyons of a tan-brown Split Mountain allured us more than any siren spirit of ancient times. We wanted to stop the car and get out to see what was what, but we had to meet Willy and make camp on the north slope of the Uintas a hundred miles farther down the road.

With steak in our bellies, we three left Vernal for Manila, thence traveled westward to Henry's Fork, via a small patch of southwestern Wyoming. On the way up into the mountains, while Willy filled us in on his experience in the Grand Gulch, we caught a glimpse of something. There in the lodgepole pines stood three or four circles of male Indians (Uintah Utes) holding hands in the dark of the night. Were they about to ghost dance? Was this the end of the world and the gathering of survivors? Their shiny black hair glistened in the moonlight. I felt a twinge of homesickness for the Wind River Indian Reservation and my old Shoshone friend Rupert Weeks, who once told me a story of his great uncles coming back from Fort Hall, Idaho, in the 1880s. On their return to Wyoming, they and others performed a ghost dance. When they all awakened the next day, they had somehow gotten five miles closer to home!

Closer to Henry's Fork, we drove slowly through an elk herd—perhaps one hundred elk pranced through the woods near the highway. Their eyes and white rumps gleamed in the lowering rays of the setting moon. Mule deer romped gracefully from tall grasses to cross our road; we had to go slow here in such a crowded assembly of wildlife. Mark spotted our turnoff for Henry's Fork, and we bounced over a dirt road into the forests of the Uintas of extreme northeastern Utah. It felt good to pull up to a campsite and even better to set up our tents and crawl into our sleeping bags in the frosty air.

The morning dawned clear but cold—ice cold. The tent had an outer layer of frost too thick to scratch off; the picnic table looked more white than brown. Was this Utah in mid-July? It sure as heck wasn't the Utah Willy had camped in a few days ago down near the Arizona line, with warm days and balmy nights. We imagined that the Earth had decided to shift its axis. As we drank our coffee, holding the mugs closely for warmth, an ungainly female moose picked her way through the willows to within forty feet of us. Even she looked cold, with her puffs of breath steaming in the air. She had a bluish tinge to her tan-gray coat.

Staring done, we packed forty pounds of gear and supplies into each of our frame packs and began a seven-mile hoof up to Dollar Lake to set up an alpine camp from which we would make our assault of Kings Peak, the highest in Utah. Within minutes we passed through bright fields of rosy paintbrushes and American bistort (whose root is edible), and on into tall stands of lodgepole pines, where we passed by delicate clusters of white geraniums and yellow arnica (whose sepals give relief from rheumatism). Gurgling streams trickled through quiet groves of aspen, where we spotted the amazingly intricate work of beavers—

neatly stacked aspen logs damming portions of feeder streams going into Henry's Fork. Enos Mills, father of Rocky Mountain National Park, wrote in *Wildlife on the Rockies* that a beaver dam was of great value in that "it spreads out or distributes the water of the few rainy days through all the days of the year. A river which flows steadily throughout the year is of inestimable value to mankind." Mills also noted, "So far as I know, the upper course of every river in the Rockies is through a number of beaver meadows, some of them acres in extent." The dams we passed by were works of art like a neatly woven carpet, providing a harbor for trout, deer, birds, and frogs—a city in the wild.

Our trail rose gently from 9,500 feet to a little over 11,000 feet over the course of seven miles. But gentle as it was, we had to give bodies frequent rests. One time we stopped on a bluff overlooking Henry's Fork stream, which flowed like silver through lodgepole pines and subalpine firs. Another time we rested on a footbridge. The icy stream gushed beneath us, soothing our minds. We began to notice the wide glacial cirques of the Uintas with maroon-colored ridges both right and left. The ridge closest to us and to our east rose steadily up to Gilbert Peak at 13,442 feet; to our west rose Flat Top Mountain at 12,170 feet. But we could not yet discern the head of the valley and Kings Peak. As western song sparrows and thrushes filled the thin air with melody, I kept thinking that we were about to enter an ancient harbor of a distant, prehistoric world.

Red Creek quartzite, for which the Uintas are famous, became more apparent the higher we climbed. According to Professor Carol Frost, some of this rock formation dates back to 2.5 billion years and more; that's more than five times older than the "ancient" Appalachians. The concept of Turtle Island hit home. The Uintas are older, more mature pieces of the ridged turtle's shell that has spread outward to Florida. Put mud on a turtle's back and the ridge lines do look like tectonic plates! Onward we forged through fir forests and across marshy meadows with globe flowers and marsh marigolds and, unfortunately, nagging mosquitoes.

Over one alpine rill, and there they rose! The high Uintas, all maroon colored with cathedral organ–shaped cliffs loomed skyward to white bands of snow and ice. We could readily discern the sedimentary layers of rock thrusted upward over millions of years ago into the pure air of over 13,000 feet. In *Basin and Range,* John McPhee asked Professor Deffeyes of Princeton University about the strange configuration of the Uintas. According to Deffeyes:

> The north side of the Uintas is a spectacular mountain wall. Glorious. You come upon it and suddenly you see structurally the boundary of the range. But you don't see what put it there. The Uintas are mysterious. They are not a basin-range fault block, yet they have come up nearly vertically, with almost no compression evident. You stand there and watch them go up into the sky. They don't fit our ideas of plate tectonics. The Rockies in general will be one of the last places in the world to be deciphered in terms of how many hits created them, and just when, and from where.

"The Uintas are mysterious" is the key. Wherever we looked, there rose masses of layered rocks, some of them looking like stepping stones to heaven. Once we had our tents set up in the woods above Dollar Lake, we ambled out into the valley to stand and stare. We could see the edge of Mount Gilbert and the flank of Flat Top Mountain and the challenging slopes of Kings Peak rising all the way up to 13,528 feet above the current seas. Kings Peak, from our vantage point, looked like the jagged edge of a tin can sticking up after being opened with a pocket knife. A small group of Boy Scouts from Salt Lake City with their leaders came trudging by.

"Have you ever climbed Kings?" I asked.

"Last year," the troop leader replied. "We didn't get back to camp till midnight, and the only way we did so was to have the kids slide down snowfields into the valley. If we had followed the trail back, we'd still be on it a year later. It's a long ways back to that peak."

"Where ya settin' up for the night?"

"Henry's Fork Lake, up yonder."

"Gonna climb Kings again?"

"Gonna try."

We knew we were in for some hard work the next day, but at least we'd be carrying only day packs, not forty-pounders. The setting sun reddened the already ruffled red ridges around us, making a perfect Martian scene—Mars with a myriad of birds, that is.

By our mosquito-ridden fire that night we ate some stew and nibbled on trail mix, all the while chatting about Kings Peak. Would we have the energy? Two of us were well over fifty. What if it poured down rain? What if it snowed? How much grub should we take up there? Should we stick to the trail all the way or try snowfields coming back down? I guess I dreamed about those questions as I fell asleep above the silvery, moonlit waters of Dollar Lake fringed with evergreens thrumming in the evening breezes.

Not so cold, I thought to myself the next morning as I scrambled out of my sleeping bag. Robins chirped just like those in my backyard in Denver. The sky? Crystal clear. And those mountains? Glorious. Mark, Willy, and I wolfed down bread and honey, cereal, and coffee and threw some oranges, bread, and candy bars into our packs. Onward and upward we paced toward Gunsight Pass at 11,800 feet. After Willy had taken several pictures, he volunteered some comments about the art of photography. He hoped to get some pieces of magic recorded on his film. Those pieces of magic in between countless other attempts are what give the photographer the impetus to keep shooting. It is a collection of those pieces of magic that the photographer gives to humankind to help in our understanding of what constitutes reality. Magical realism is not something out of Latin American fiction, where mythological realities fuse with daily reality. It could be a Mormon Fritillary butterfly fertilizing an alpine blossom with his fuzzy antennae in the high Uintas—a kind of moth-person like a kachina spirit helping keep alive our green planet.

"What could it be?" I asked out loud.

"It could be almost anything," Willy responded. A magical moment makes a reality that has as much verisimilitude as Henry James's notion of realism. The notion of verisimilitude has to take in meta-realities beyond drawing-room conversation. What is meta-reality? Geology, for one thing, and mythology for another. It is like the distant siren a canine hears or the faint grinding of tectonic plates a panda bear detects just before an earthquake, or the vision of survivors who will gather in the Uintas.

Gunsight Pass rose just ahead as we cleared the last scrubby stands of fragrant spruce and fir. At last we rambled over Utah tundra, our first ever in that state. Mark gleefully pointed down to some white alpine forget-me-nots, usually blue in color. Alpine sunflowers, the largest flower of the tundra, all pointed eastward toward the rising sun. Clusters of dwarf, blue columbines hid among the dark crevices of trailside rocks. The air up here was exhilarating; each breathful was elixir to our lungs. No real clouds accumulated westward yet, and Gilbert Peak looked so clear that you could stretch your arm across Gunsight Pass and touch it. A few switchbacks and two snowfields later, we sat down at windy Gunsight Pass to eat a candy bar with no middle-aged qualms of guilt about how fattening chocolate-caramel is.

From up here we could see northward to the flat stretches of green plains and brown desert of my old home state of Wyoming. Somewhere out there, perhaps a Basque shepherd glanced up into the rugged Uintas and the cool white snowfields at our sides. Each vantage point offered new meta-realities. To the south spread glacial valleys and winding ridges down to the heart of the Uintah and Ouray Indian Reservation, so completely different from the landscape of Ute Mountain Reservation down Mesa Verde way. The boundaries of this more northern reservation now extend approximately to where we sat. We could not see Kings Peak, as a cathedral organ–shaped mountain blocked our view. Pipits winged past us, resisting the forceful gusts of wind and making for moments of magic on the film of our brains. If I had been a pipit, I don't know that I could have had any control in all the wind with my fluttering gray feathers. Time to move on.

We followed the spongy, wet trail to Anderson Pass and Kings Peak. But the trail descended! We did not want to go down, just to go up again. Nonetheless, we didn't wish to scramble across loose scree to a possible dead end high above and therefore dutifully followed the trail down to an alluring meadowland full of flowers and willows and trickling brooks. The soil had become even more spongy, and we hopped like toads through stygian lands dwarfed by the massive peaks of an upper world. The smell of fresh plants permeated our valley. Thoreau described the scents of a New England marsh in his *Journal:*

> I perceive some of that peculiar fragrance from the marsh at the Hubbard Causeway, though the marsh is mostly covered. It has a particular compound of odors. It is more remarkable and memorable than the scent of any particular plant,—the fragrance, as it were, of the earth itself.

We took a shortcut through the marsh by heading directly toward Anderson Pass, once we determined its location to the northwest. Kings Peak looked impossibly rocky and gigantic. I even suggested following a contour line up the back side of the mountain instead of going all the way to Anderson Pass, but upon closer examination, my suggested route appeared to be absolutely treacherous.

No clouds yet. Now began our uphill trek to Anderson Pass. It reminded me somewhat of the pathway up Medicine Bow Peak near Laramie, Wyoming, which my family and I had taken each Labor Day for twelve years straight. But Anderson Pass rests considerably above 12,000 feet, and the very top of Medicine Bow Peak is barely over 12,000 feet. We knew that once we stood on Anderson Pass, our troubles would begin. We would have a whole mountain to climb. My water supply (as at the Grand Canyon) was getting a bit low, and I should never have taken a piece of sweet candy from Mark; it made me intolerably thirsty. I felt that I was losing energy fast, and Anderson Pass looked miles away. Thankfully, we all stopped for a much-needed rest by potable rivulets of icy snowmelt coming off Kings Peak.

Within several hundred feet, the tundra leveled off again, and thankfully, the going was easier. In fact, I led the way to the base of a large snowfield just below Anderson Pass. Here we ate lunch, although I was more thirsty than hungry. We looked down on the valley containing Dollar Lake and the head-waters of Henry's Fork River and could see the incredibly steep chute the Boy Scouts had slid down the year before. We felt the chill of the snowfield and proceeded onward, if only to warm up. Cautiously, we picked our steps through watermelon-smelling snow (thoroughly laced with a poisonous-to-humans red algae known as *Chlamydomonas nivalis).* Willy was the first to make it to the top of the pass.

"Hey, we're at 12,700 feet!" Willy shouted.

"Are you sure it isn't 12,200 feet?" I asked.

"Read the sign!"

Truly we all stood at 12,700 feet, some 500 feet higher than I had expected. That information gave me a boost. We had only 828 vertical feet to go—a mere eighty-story building the likes of the Chrysler Building in New York City.

Thankfully, there was still no sign of clouds over that vast Utah sky. Willy got a kick out of my newfound energy and bounded ahead, picking his way along a barely visible trail, over loose slabs of shale shining in the sun and darker granite boulders. It's one thing to follow a winding trail over tundra and quite another to make rapid progress up rock cliffs, past dizzying overhangs, with nothing but sky all around.

High pitched squeaks of pikas filled the air as Utah spread before us. We could begin to make out the distant, swirling canyons of Split Mountain back on the Colorado border. Had some sort of massive swirling motion caused the east-west orientation of the Uintas? We glanced down at the High Line Trail, winding over pass and gorge, running the length of the Uintas. At one point it looked as narrow as a pathway out to Bright Angel Point in the Grand Canyon. The trail snaked along an almost vertical pitch on the back side of Red Castle Mountain. One miscalculation and you'd be history. Willy and I stopped to make sure Mark was coming along all right. When he waved, we proceeded up to a false summit, only to see the high, jagged block of Kings still a ways up there.

Although there were not as many flowers around us as there were on the tundra, the beauty and diversity of the rocks made up for it. We could see in any direction granites, shales, quartzites, and sandstones, all with a reddish-brown hue. Deep within the rocks we could hear the gurgle of underground springs and streams as though we stood on icy Mount Rainier. We wondered if there was a network of watery channels inside possible caverns? Such is the case with the Wasatch Range and its Timpanogos Cave. Willy tried to capture pieces of magic by stopping here and there to compose photographs ever so carefully, sometimes ever so precariously, near the western edge of Kings Peak high above the linear geosynclines of the Uintas.

It was fun working our way up to the summit. There were ample grips on the rocks above. Each little chimney gained meant another thirty or forty vertical feet. We knew the mountain couldn't go on forever and at last stood at a spot where there was more sky than land. A plaque, honoring Clarence King as the first director of the US Geological Survey, marked the highest point in Utah, although many peaks looked equally high. One tired climber just back from South Kings told us not to be fooled—Kings is clearly higher. He had been fooled. From up here we could see a cluster of peaks all over 13,000 feet, including South Kings, Gilbert, Emmons, and Red Knob. The high, snowy, cone-shaped summit by the name of Tokewanna Peak, at 13,123 feet, gleamed to the west. When Mark arrived at the top, he stretched out on a flat boulder of the turtle's shell and took a nice nap as though he rested on a hammock in his own backyard. Perhaps that was the highest nap he had ever taken, and the most enjoyable, judging from the smile on his face. This hour on the rugged, jagged summit made for what John Muir called "pure mountaineity."

A new alpine melody started brewing for us. To the west, Tokewanna Peak darkened with bolts of lightning thrashing its flanks. Distant thunder awakened Mark, and we three descended rather quickly over loose slabs, wobbly rocks, slippery snow, and rocking boulders. Another storm brewed to the south toward Vernal, with prehistoric forks of lightning stabbing the sky. But overhead, strangely enough, it remained clear and sunny. Arriving at Anderson Pass, our knees felt wobbly; even Willy, some twenty years younger, sat down for a rest just above the snowfield. Nonetheless, going down seemed quicker and easier.

We hopped and skipped down the snowfield we had so gingerly stepped up hours ago. I wished I had a pair of skis to swoosh down like an eagle to the little snow buttercups just blooming at the snowy base. Melting snow rolled in torrents down our trail, forcing us to skim the tops of boulders to the side. Pipits and rosy finches pursued their insect prey, sometimes almost brushing our shoulders. Thunder boomed to the south and west, but it looked like we would remain storm-free as the clouds sliced away from us. Meanwhile, Willy clicked away, busier than a cat chasing a butterfly.

At last we descended into the sunny meadow below Gunsight Pass. I managed to slip and catch myself with my hands as I fell sharply to the stony earth. A few drops of blood ran from the palm of my hand, reddening the already red Uintas. It felt good to soak my hand in a cold stream and press some watercress against the scratch. We stopped to chat with some campers in the high meadow who wondered how long it would take to get to the top of Kings the next day.

"A lot easier than from Dollar Lake," we said.

Then came our ascent back up to Gunsight Pass. This was hard work after climbing Kings—so hard that I rested every hundred yards until I found a snowbank free of red algae. I quickly brushed aside the dirty surface to get down to a pure white inner layer and made myself a snow cone containing a few harder hail pellets; quickly my energy returned as at the Grand Canyon.

"I hope you got a few pieces of magic, Willy."

"Yeah, I think so, but you know what Ansel Adams said—negatives are only the beginning. They are the musical score, but making the print is the performance of that score. I got a lot of work ahead of me. There are lots of things you can do to enhance a print in a darkroom, to highlight a shining flower in the sun."

"Sort of like editing a rough draft of an essay, right Willy?"

"Sort of."

By six o'clock in the evening we had Gunsight Pass behind us as we three plodded along the trail through tundra and krummholz to Dollar Lake, mosquitoes and all. Noodles in Alfredo sauce never tasted better, and so, too, did slices of dark bread and dried apricots, apples, and peaches boiled to perfection. We used the fruit-flavored boiling water (once the fruit was gone) to make hot tea; this new camp-side invention proved to be superb, even with an occasional floating mosquito.

Dollar Lake's waters soon reflected the moon, and three weary guys turned in for the night. I guess I dreamed of a ghost dance and woke up startled in the middle of the night. Echoing off the cliff sides of our valley came the eerie, loud, high-pitched bugling of several elk. I listened for a few minutes and dozed off into a deep sleep in the high Uintas, an ancient continent within a continent, west-running though it was. The next morning we all felt a touch of sadness as we shouldered our heavy packs for our descent to the valley below.

II—Elbert

Three of us—Mark Reames, my son Rich, and I—got out of work too late to set up camp at Half Moon Creek later that night. Instead, we bunked at a motel in Leadville two miles above sea level. Winds whipped the streets of Leadville that chilly September evening, forcing us to make a quick retreat to our room. We spread out our map of the Mount Elbert region and looked for the dotted line of the trail that led to the second highest peak in the lower forty-eight states. At 14,433 feet, Mount Elbert is only sixty-one feet lower than Mount Whitney that rises so high above Death Valley. Our trail would merge briefly with the Colorado Trail that skirts the Rockies from Wyoming to New Mexico. It was too cold even inside the motel to stay up too long looking at maps, and we turned in to sleep soundly until 6 A.M.

The morning of September 11 proved to be fantastically clear—so clear that Leadville looked as though it would be swallowed up by the lurking summits of Mounts Elbert and Massive, laced in snow. By 8 A.M. we had our packs on and proceeded at a rapid pace on the trail above Half Moon Creek campground. Drooping aspen had already turned in color to a light yellow. Their leaves rustled with each gentle breeze, sounding like a ceremonial gourd. The usual suspects of Canada jays and Clark's nutcrackers squawked loudly as we trudged by. Within an hour we reached tree line at 11,500 feet, some 10,000 feet higher than it is in subarctic Iceland. But it was so chilly, we retreated to a clump of dwarfed spruces to put on sweaters and parkas and eat a bit of trail mix followed with swigs of water.

We proceeded more slowly out onto the windswept tundra, noticing that the late summer sunflowers had wilted to the ground. In fact, the entire grassy tundra appeared rust-colored in contrast with greener ranch lands below. We thought we spotted the summit looming far above and slowed our pace down a bit more now that we had reached the 13,000-foot level. Rich pointed to the valleys below, with golden and glowing aspen groves looking like tongues of fire in narrow valleys. We had to keep moving in this brisk and chilly air. After a half hour or so of huffing and puffing, we reached what we thought was the summit, only to see yet more summits rising in the distance. Somehow this discouragement slowed me down all the more. In fact, I stopped and rested more than usual, unlike my experience at Anderson Pass where I felt rejuvenated on Kings Peak. After a few swigs of canteen water, I crawled along at a snail's pace up over windswept, rocky crests. Mark, perhaps out of empathy, slowed his pace down to mine. We trekked along a more level spot but at an altitude higher than the summit of Longs Peak. Breathing became a bit difficult. My son, more than thirty years younger, decided to forge ahead and wait for us somewhere way up above.

Mark and I slowed down considerably as we crossed a fresh snowfield ankle-deep. At 14,300 feet, we stopped and rested. Neither of us had been this high before. The mountain seemed to be freaking me out. At last, we saw a second higher hump and yet an even higher summit crested with snow and people all gathered around looking like tiny grasshoppers. The hike from the second false summit to the true summit above 14,400 feet reminded me a bit of the final approach to Kings Peak, with its nice, sheer views down to a bald glacial bowl to the west.

At last we met Rich at the true summit, where he had been waiting anxiously for us for forty-five minutes. We signed the register and sat down behind some rocks out of the wind to snack on oranges, rice cakes, and, of all things, fresh tomatoes (sprinkled with salt) from Mark's garden. We stood up again to stare into space and a phenomenal view to the south past icy La Plata Peak to the Sangre de Cristo Range. To our west rose the incredibly white Snowmass Peak and the Eiger-faced Capitol Peak. To the east and north we could clearly make out Pikes Peak and Longs Peak, both two to three hundred feet lower. We took one last glance around and ambled back down, hoping our knees wouldn't give out on a very steep and long descent, all the way back to Half Moon Creek of the lowlands only two miles above sea level as opposed to nearly three miles above the oceans.

III—San Francisco Peaks

Imagine a black volcano fleeced with snow clouds that clear momentarily to reveal three jagged crests as white as Antarctica. Imagine those clouds spreading eastward in an early June sky to shed rain on a young corn crop of a Hopi mesa. The range, known as the San Francisco Peaks of northern Arizona, has a mystical air about it, and for that reason alone we wished to climb it. The Hopi people of Arizona believe that ancient kachina spirits reside atop the San Francisco Peaks for a portion of the year. During the summer, the spirits become rain clouds and spread out from the mountain to three of their mesas in the desert. These life-giving clouds help corn mature to furnish food for both body and spirit throughout the rest of the year. The Hopi believe that when you eat corn, you can intuit the story of their existence. The mountain is clearly a sacred part of that story, as are kachina spirits (more than 160 different ones), which teach human beings the art of desert survival.

Three of us left Denver in late May by way of New Mexico to Flagstaff, Arizona. We hoped it would not be too early to attempt an ascent of the four-million-year-old volcano's summit, which rises to the highest point in Arizona at 12,633 feet. We knew there would be snow, judging from the amount of shiny white stuff on the Sangre de Cristos of northern New Mexico; we sensed that it might even be tough going. But we were determined—so determined that we prepared ourselves with practice climbs of three other mountains before setting out on the Kachina Wilderness Trail outside Flagstaff.

Spending our first night in a friend's adobe home in the heart of the desert south of Santa Fe, we soon found ourselves bouncing along a forest service road going up Grandmother Spider Mountain (*Tse-pi'na*—Taylor Mountain) near Grants, New Mexico. Arriving on a high, windy plateau, Willy Sutton, Mark Reames, and I took swigs of water, shouldered our packs, and quickly paced along an ascending trail through groves of aspen mixed with Douglas fir. The trail underfoot was soft and spongy.

Laguna Pueblo author Leslie Marmon Silko refers to this mountain numerous times in her writings, particularly in her novel *Ceremony*. She has this to say about it: "She [Grandmother Spider Mountain] waited in certain locations for people to come to her for help. She alone had known how to outsmart the malicious mountain Kat'sina who imprisoned rain clouds in the northwest room of his magical house. . . ." This ancient spider had told a timeless mythical figure "Sun Man to win the storm clouds back…so they would be free again to bring rain and snow to the people." The spider is sacred to the southwestern tribes. She taught humans the principle of weaving, whether carpet or story. For that matter, all animals have something to teach us, be they three ants sharing the burden of carrying food with their strong-as-iron mandibles, or beavers thumping a warning with their tails when a tree they have chiseled is about to fall, or pocket gophers standing straight up to squeak out a warning that a rattlesnake is in the area.

But to return to our trail—we emerged from the aspen groves and firs onto slanting fields with clumps of grass that had the feel and look of Irish thatched cottages. The *malpais* (bad country) of dark lava fanned out on the valley floor far below, glistening in the sun (as though it was still steaming), many hundreds of thousands of years ago. Grandmother Spider Mountain last erupted perhaps a million years ago in Mount Saint Helens's fashion—blowing its stack from its side. Arms of lava (now covered with trees and grasses) finger outward from the peak like dark spider webs. Far above us lay snowfields tucked in the flank of the peak. We paused to watch a mountain bluebird flutter above the grasses, lending itself as a patch of blue to an otherwise cloudy sky. Chickadees sang out from a fringe of pines as we crisscrossed the grassy hummocks. We had the sensation of walking inside a landscape painting of Paul Cezanne set at 11,000 feet. Thunderheads built up to the west toward the Arizona line as we approached the base of the snowfield that rose some thirty feet to the peak itself. Perhaps Grandmother Spider was up to her old tricks of liberating clouds from the trickster Kat'sina.

Since the snow lay at a steep angle, we opted for an exposed rocky crevice, and in five minutes, we stood atop the spider's cephalothorax with spinnerets of elk sedge, currant bushes, and Indian rice grass. From up here at 11,600 feet, we could gaze at a third of the state of New Mexico with most of the Pueblo villages for which this sacred spider means so much—a great rain cloud collector. Leslie Silko's Laguna Pueblo lay east-southeast. Acoma Pueblo, home of the Native American author Simon Ortiz, loomed southward. Santa Clara Pueblo, home of Maria the potter, lay to the northeast in the Rio Grande Valley. And far to the south lay N. Scott Momaday's Jemez Pueblo, setting for his Pulitzer Prize–winning novel *House Made of Dawn*, and some passages in *The Way to Rainy Mountain*. To our north rose a spruce hummock with taller, more sheltered trees in the middle, similar to the forests of the savanna in the American Southeast. A steady wind buffeted us from an oncoming storm.

Webs of clouds began to collect in the lower valleys, and as the clouds from Arizona closed in, we could readily imagine our spider mountain catching some thunderheads. In *Ceremony,* Silko describes Tse-pi'na as "spinning out of the thunderheads like gray spider webs and tangling against the foothills of the mountain. Scott Momaday writes in *The Way to Rainy Mountain:*

> In New Mexico the land is made of many colors.
> When I was a boy I rode out over the red and
> Yellow and purple earth west of Jemez
> Pueblo . . . I know what it is, on a hot day in
> August or September, to ride into a bank of cold,
> Fresh rain.

We, too, rode into a bank of cold rain as we rolled along eastern Arizona highways, leaving Tse-pi'na far behind.

We arranged for a rendezvous with two friends from Pennsylvania to climb the San Francisco Peaks, but after talking with them on the phone at a pit stop, we became a little apprehensive. They informed us that a freak blizzard had dumped four feet of fresh snow, trapping some climbers high up on Humphreys Peak, the tallest of the San Francisco Peaks. Rescue parties succeeded in getting all stranded people off the mountain. Should we dare try it?

"Let's meet anyway at the Snow Bowl Trailhead tomorrow," I told Gordon and Walt Fader.

Thirty-four years earlier, Gordon and I relived Henry David Thoreau's adventure by climbing Mount Katahdin above the black spruce forests of northern Maine. Here in Arizona, we picked a camping spot under the Strawberry Volcano, which flanked the northeast slope of the very snowy San Francisco Peaks. Was the fresh snow really four feet deep? How deep was the older snow underneath? More clouds gathered that evening, looking like Chinese lanterns all lit up with thrashing heat lightning. A bit ominous, I thought to myself; we all read each other's mind. Thunder rattled in the distance like drums at some kachina ceremony. One last beer by the cozy campfire and we turned in, encouraged by the appearance of a star or two.

About four in the morning, a scattered group of coyotes yelped, but it was too early to get up. I went back to sleep until a little before 5:30 A.M. The coyotes were still yelping on a clear and glorious morning. Breakfast wolfed down, we headed for Strawberry Volcano to get a little practice before ascending the Kachina Spirits Mountain with the Faders or by ourselves the following day. Not a cloud in the sky—except for wisps around the upper snowfields. Strawberry Volcano loomed above us the opposite way, with black and red cinders touching the sky. Mark Reames and I, who had both lived in Japan, couldn't help but think of Fuji San with all that black, pebbly ash spewed out from the lip of the crater. Willy was already racing up the steep slope a hundred yards ahead of us. Bright-green cabbage-like plants grew right out of the lava ash all the way upslope, looking just like a Georgia O'Keeffe painting. There's something about the desert that gets you. It's a kind of outer space on Earth. Green plants, black soil, red lava, blue sky, and a touch of white cloud make for stark austerity. Amid the volcanic starkness, we at last stood atop the rim of Strawberry Volcano.

It, too, had exploded outward from its eastward side several thousand years ago (much more recently than the San Francisco Peaks), leaving a crescent form to face the rising sun. But within the crescent stood a half dozen Anasazi dwellings made of red blocks of lava. Since this volcano remained active until a thousand years ago, these ancient people lived within earshot of hissing steam vents. Down lower, they built retainer walls for rich black earth in which to grow yellow squash, white and red corn, and golden melons. How fantastic a village it must have been under a strong sun or a starry night with flickering open-pit fires! Did they make use of hissing steam vents for heat in the winter as Icelanders do now?

The rising sun's rays glinted brightly off these Anasazi ruins, giving them a life of their own and extending their spirits into our tired century. The coyotes continued to yip-yap in the distance. Their presence in the Old West certainly engendered many a story. There is an old Hispanic legend about a Señor Coyote, and it goes like this. A rattler had a huge boulder fall on him while he was napping, but fortunately for the snake, a rabbit hopped by. He begged the rabbit to free him from the boulder. The rabbit complied, only to have the liberated snake announce that the rabbit would be his dinner for the day. However, Señor Coyote came along and the rabbit appealed to him for justice. The snake defended himself by saying that the rabbit had rolled the boulder on him in the first place and certainly he deserved to be eaten. The coyote pretended that it was too complicated for him to understand and that they should reenact the story. When the snake was safely under the rock again, crushed in pain, Señor Coyote said, "*Pues* (well then), I guess you're stuck and that must be your reward for trying to eat the rabbit after he had treated you with such kindness."

It was now 6:30 A.M. and time to dash down the scree, a feat accomplished in minutes. We didn't encounter any snakes or rabbits but continued to hear coyotes as we left three sets of tracks in the cinders en route to rendezvous with the Faders. Gordon and Walt arrived at the Snow Bowl with worried looks on their faces. They definitely did not wish to hike up through waist-deep snow to be rescued by a medevac chopper. We had planned in advance to make the ascent the following day and teased them a little about going up to investigate. We finally consented to climb a lesser mountain near Sedona called Wilson Mountain, named after some poor soul who was gobbled alive by a grizzly bear in the nineteenth century.

Although there was no threat of snow, there were other hazards that didn't seem to bother the Faders. From their hiking information sheet, I quote:

> HAZARDS—we do have various rattlesnake species throughout the area, so STAY ALERT! Coral snakes, also venomous, are listed for our area, mainly in the higher elevations (where we were going), but sightings are extremely rare. You are more apt to see a king snake (non-venomous, but will bite), which is often mistaken for the coral snake—scorpions, centipedes, and black widow spiders may also be encountered—Do not expose your hands, arms, or legs by placing them into spots where you can't see.

Sure beats snow!

We five put on our packs, filled our canteens, and marched out single file along a trail shimmering in heat. There wasn't the slightest trace of snow, but who knows? The beauty of this trail winding its way up Mount Wilson soon got to us. A pinyon jay scrambled through the clear air from pine branch to juniper shrub upslope, leading our eyes toward jagged red pinnacles of dark and lighter sandstone mixed with very dark bands of basalt glaring in the sun. This terrain looked exactly like Edward Abbey's kind of country.

Numerous century plants, the first I'd ever seen, punctuated the brown hills with sixteen-foot stalks weighed down with bright red buds that were about to burst open into white blossoms—an event that occurs infrequently, perhaps once every hundred years. But since each plant had bloomed in a different sequence, any given desert slope could have a few, out of many, blooming. Heavily podded yucca plants scattered themselves on the open ground in and around the century plants. Yep, this sure was Abbey country!

Desert tribes not only admired the beauty of the yucca plant, but, as we have seen in the Grand Gulch, made use of it for sandals from its fibrous roots. They made soap from the yucca's roots mixed with water, fruit from its pods, necklaces from its black seeds, and food from the youngest tender roots, which taste something like a strong carrot.

No snakes or spiders so far, and definitely no snow. But we were thirsty. Consequently, we often paused to take a drink and sprinkle water on our heads. "We could have been in waist-deep snow," I said to Gordon with a twinkle in my eye. He (we) looked mighty hot, but we were gaining altitude and catching the faintest breeze from the wooded ridges above. A melodious canyon warbler trilled through the pinnacled canyons around us, but we could not echolocate him. Soon we stood on a ledge where earth met sky and moths met the yellow blossoms of knee-high prickly pear cactus. By now, a few shrubs of service-berry graced the trailside, along with manzanita bushes that had crabapple-sized fruit, sometimes green, sometimes with a blush of red. Breeze or no breeze, it remained mighty hot, and I had to take a few swallows more of tepid canteen water.

"Let's try and make it to the saddle above for lunch," Mark suggested.

We all grunted our consent and trudged several hundred feet higher until at last we rested our bones on light-green, lichen-covered rocks. We all simultaneously grabbed some oranges that were stowed in our backpacks; we peeled our oranges faster than a rattler's strike and savored each juicy morsel. Willy, with half an orange in his mouth, began to take black-and-white images of the stark landscapes below the saddle. Above us rose massive Wilson Mountain, silhouetted by stalks of red pods that rose ridiculously high above the century plant. It was time for cheese and jalapeño-pepper bread, but not too much with my limited water supply.

"Hey, Willy—here's something you should photograph," we said, pointing to Wilson Mountain from behind a century plant.

"You don't take setups like that," Willy said. "Otherwise you're taking pictures of your own ideas. Too much is happening out there for you to bother with setups. You gotta let things happen."

He did take a shot of Wilson Mountain, but just as a cloud shadow touched its surface. We raised our weary bones and proceeded along the trail into a mixed aspen–Douglas fir forest. It started to rain. It cooled us and we felt good. As the mist rose from the warm forest floor, I imagined I was in Rwanda looking for gorillas in the bush. Jays squawked in the temporary rain forest of Arizona. In the deep woods, just below the summit, we spotted a rufous-sided towhee and heard the high-pitched cheep of the bush tit. I really liked this gently rising forest. Manzanita bushes grew everywhere, and even wild strawberries.

The top of Wilson Mountain was flat, very flat. We hoofed through pleasant woods but looked for a break in the trees to get a view. We plodded onward until Walt Fader, running on ahead, found the trail's terminus. He stood in the distance, staring. No wonder. When we arrived at the edge of the cliff, all we could do was look down to endless gargoyles of colored sandstone. Two ravens followed the thermals in front of us. Vincent Van Gogh would have gone mad here. The heck with cornfields and crows in Arles! Meanwhile, we had our own artist going mad. Willy did an Apache mountain spirits dance within our midst, clicking his camera everywhere—not anywhere, but everywhere suitable. We took mental snapshots of the kind that won't fade, especially of the manzanita bushes in pink bloom perched at the dizzying edge of an 800-foot drop-off into a pink sandstone infinity.

Thunder rumbled, and we moved on to another part of the mountain, facing north and away from the storm to gaze at the distant and ever-so white San Francisco Peaks (*Nuvatukyaovi,* or home of the kachina spirits) and tomorrow's climb. We could see that this mountain also blew its stack from the side in Mount Saint Helens's fashion but two million years ago. Western meadowlarks and song sparrows spewed out rich pieces of dissolved land-scapes with their melodious notes, flavored with yucca and sage. In bright sun, we stretched out for a bit of a nap, not worrying one iota about venomous coral snakes. Why should we worry, with their reputation of being seldom seen? However—lucky me—when I rolled in my sleepiness, I felt the sudden sting of a fang against my left knee. Fortunately, it was only a yucca plant. Nonetheless, my knee throbbed as much as if it had been a snakebite. By the time we made our descent to the heat of the lower vales, my knee no longer hurt and my spirit soared in the company of my friends amid the stark desert landscape. It was sad to see the hand-waving Faders fade into the distance, making the present reality seem like a dream. Had we really climbed a moun-tain with them?

We camped that night on a high, windy flank of the inner basin, a deep valley within the volcanic caldera of the San Francisco Peaks. Under a moonless sky we dozed off, listening to the wind in the pines. I dreamed of my daughter's new apartment in Hoboken, New Jersey. I was still lugging furniture up ten flights of stairs, thinking how this would be good practice for climbing the highest peaks in Arizona. I looked out my daughter's window up on the fifth floor to see patches of green sycamore trees amid rows of brownstone apartments and shops. Somewhere out there was Nelson's Marine Bar, where a desert rat named Edward Abbey hung out between his lengthy stays in the canyon lands of Utah. Where in the world is Nelson's Marine Bar . . . ?

"Rise and shine," Willy shouted. "Coffee's on!" Somehow it had become early morning and time to get moving.

By 7 A.M. we stood at the Sun Bowl Trailhead, looking up at an incredibly white Humphreys Peak, highest of the volcanic pinnacles. The sky was an intense blue with just a few wisps of clouds billowing over icy snowfields. It looked like the snow dropped well down into the upper forests—how far down we couldn't quite tell. Written on yesterday's register (May 31, 1992) was a message from a German climbing party that was simple and clear: "Snow too deep—had to turn around."

"But that was yesterday," said Mark with a gleam in his eye.

We secured our packs and ambled at a comfortable pace through sweet-smelling, peaceful aspen groves. The creamy white trunks rose thick and straight. The branches quaked with myriad trembling leaves that looked like quivering feathers on a kachina dancer. The upper canopy of this aspen grove turned the sunlight green. No snow yet! Our gentle trail slowly zigzagged skyward, and aspen gave way to Douglas fir. Westerly vistas spread before us, revealing dozens of inactive volcanic humps. You'd think at least one of them would still be active, but nary a one. Trekking onward through columns of fir and pine, we began to feel the spirit of this mountain tug at us as rain clouds spread eastward toward the three Hopi mesas.

I remember once buying a beautiful freestanding hummingbird kachina doll (blossom fertilizer) in a pawnshop in Casper, Wyoming. It was an old doll, as the cottonwood root from which it was carved was splitting, and its green, bearded ruff had faded considerably. Because it was freestanding, it must have been made around 1950 or earlier. This doll, like many others, somehow got sold in the market instead of being burnt up to ashes, as it should have been. These colorful wooden dolls were once used solely as teaching devices, and once the Hopi child learned which kachina spirit this particular doll represented, the doll was destroyed by fire. I had this marvelous doll as part of my collection from 1976 until we moved to an apartment in Denver in 1990, when it, along with others, was stolen. At first I was mortified that I could no longer claim this unique spiritual curiosity as mine. Upon reflection, I realized how foolish I was to assume that this kachina doll was mine and only mine. I knew all along it should have been destroyed, because it had served its purpose as a wooden symbol of a powerful spirit. Thank you, whoever you are, for separating me from this most touchable replica.

Erna Fergusson described Hopi dancers getting ready early in the morning for imploring kachina spirits to bring rain clouds:

> Peering over the rocks, we could see the dancers gathered on a flat stretch of sand sheltered by an overhanging rock. They were already dressed in dance kirtles and sashes, fringed brown moccasins, and flaring shirts of pinyon boughs. Their bodies were smeared with corn-smut, a sort of dare to the gods to send rain and wash it off. On each torso were interlocking crescents done in white paint, symbols of friendship. The gaudy masks sat in a row on the rocks, waiting, and looking curiously human.

By now, at 9,000 feet or so, we encountered our first small patches of snow. They got deeper when the trail passed through ravines. Just on the upper side of one of these ravines, we paused for some water and a little trail mix. A young woman from Phoenix stopped to chat, saying she had never encountered so much snow this late in the season (it was only June 1, and no Colorado mountain worth its salt could be climbed this early without winter gear). She asked if it was okay to accompany us, and the four of us climbed merrily in the deepening snow until we came to a lava flow, where the trail seemed to end. The girl waited while we proceeded to climb the green, lichen-covered lava to look for the continuation of the trail. No luck. What happened to it? The girl shouted that she had discovered the switchback was right where she sat, and that we all had missed it. She went on with another climbing party while we gingerly descended the wobbly lava flow, all the while looking at the barely green quaking aspen forests far below.

Erna Fergusson wrote:

> As the dancers climbed over the rocks, we saw first the feathers and spires of headed grass which topped the masks. Each mask is in itself a cloud symbol and bears many symbols of cloud and rain and a rainbow on its terraced top. At the back of each one a small Kachina doll stood on a carved ear of corn or on another Kachina. Around the neck was a ruff of spruce, a Kachina symbol, and each man carried spruce in one hand, the inevitable rattle in the other. Jingling and talking, they appeared, first the gay-colored masks, then the men, a long line. They stopped a moment at a shrine built of slabs of rock, added their quota of meal to the white scatterings already there, and then moved on across the causeway.

Clouds gathered in from the west, but they were not the least bit threatening. The snow deepened among the aisles of spruce, and the Phoenix girl was on her way back. "Too much snow," she said, "but keep on following the tracks to the right. The couple I was with is determined to make it." Sometimes we sank up to our knees in fresh and glittering snow, but for the most part, the three of us carefully edged our way skyward. At one point, the trail of footprints went straight upslope, with no zigzags. This proved to be tiresome above 10,000 feet, especially when you didn't know if you would break through snow and sink up to your hips as I did once trying to climb Sandia Crest above Albuquerque one February day.

Fergusson poetically continued:

The maskers danced first in the narrow plaza in front of the first house in Walpi. The first movement was simple: rhythmic pounding of feet in perfect time, as the bodies swing now right, now left, showing front and back views of the weird masks, the swishing skirts. All the time dancers sang, catching without error the frequent changes in tempo. To and fro they swung, to and fro, following the leader's chant, intoning the deep droning prayer, curiously muffled under masks.

At the top of this steep hill, we raised our canteens and gurgled cold water down our dry gullets and ate a handful of trail mix. We could begin to see the Snow Bowl Ski Area to our right and heard, and finally saw, a three-toed woodpecker jackhammering a dead spruce in search of insects. A chickaree squirrel chattered upslope somewhere, and ravens flew overhead, convincing us of the fitness of the name "San Francisco Peaks" in honor of the twelfth-century Saint Francis of Assisi, who loved animals of all kinds. St. Francis wrote a charming small volume called *Little Flowers*, in which he recorded his tender words for turtle doves, which he prevented from being sold as food: "O my little sisters, simple, innocent, pure doves, why have you let yourselves be caught? Now I wish to save you from death and make nests for you, so that you can be fruitful and multiply as God your Maker ordained." This mountain wilderness remains a perpetual nest for wildlife.

Our trail of scant footprints led to the northern edge of the Snow Bowl (not part of the wilderness area), where we caught our first glimpse of wintry Agassiz Peak, rising above like one of the Himalayas. Agassiz Peak is reserved for Hopi People only as it is considered to be the sacred residence of kachina spirits. It looked so high above us we wondered whether we would ever make it to the volcanic rim. Some of us began to have secret doubts. God, it was a long ways up there. At last we came to the couple who had made tracks ahead of us.

"This is it," they said. "The snow has completely obliterated the trail and the snow is soft and slippery." But there was another option—loose volcanic scree served as a pathway to the sky. "I know what yer thinking," one of the climbers said. "But that stuff is as loose as hell. I wouldn't try it if I were you." But that was like speaking to a stone wall (no pun intended). We had to do it—that's why we came here. We just had to do it.

Erna Fergusson wrote:

> Then they stopped and stood at ease while the leaders prepared for the second movement. First they arranged on the ground a row of folded blankets, dirty quilts, whatever they had or whatever women threw down from the housetops. On these the seven women figures knelt, facing the men. In front of each woman was a hollow gourd, and each one wielded the deer scapula to bring out a hollow squawking, so perfect in rhythm as not to be unpleasant. Chanting, the Kachinas danced to this music, the steps a little more vigorous than in the first figure.

We three began our scramble up loose scree. It was so black that hardly any snow remained, so strong was the June sun. At first it seemed like fun, but after a half hour or so of losing our footing, sliding backward every time we pushed forward, and seeing very little progress in total elevation gained, we realized we were in for some difficult work. Sometimes harder ledges of lava gave us firmer footholds and handholds, and sometimes we had to cross loose volcanic gravel that put everything into slow motion, as in a dream. The snowy forest that skirted the edge of the lava flow gradually thinned out to mere dwarfs. We could no longer spot the two climbers below, as everything merged with the gigantic Snow Bowl and Agassiz Peak.

Now halfway up the lip of the volcano, we paused (each at a different level in space) to take a drink of cool water. Just as I stood up to forge onward, two air force jets buzzed the edge of the volcanic rim no more than a thousand feet above us, their thunderous roar frightening us and causing us almost to lose our footing. My first reaction of fear rapidly transformed to anger. Was not this sacred mountain part of the Kachina Wilderness Area? Is there not a sufficient number of lesser volcanoes the jets could buzz? Why buzz a wilderness area? Congress must see to it that wilderness areas be left in peace and not be abused by military jets. Such practice must cease.

The Wilderness Act of 1964, signed by President Lyndon Johnson, states:

> A designated wilderness is an area of underdeveloped Federal land set aside by Congress and administered for the enjoyment of the public, scientific research, scenic, and historic values. This is accomplished in a manner so as to leave it unimpaired for future generations. More specifically, we define wilderness as a relatively large natural area that is neither easily accessible nor frequented by motorized vehicles. The wilderness is an area where opportunities exist for primitive activities not readily apparent.

So states the forest service handout entitled "The Kachina Peaks–Inner Basin Wilderness Guide." A military jet is a motorized vehicle that impairs the enjoyment of the public.

The upper third of the lava flow proved to be less tiresome than the first section just above the trail. In fact, up at timberline or a little below, we picked up the trail once again, which wound its way through hummocks of bristlecone pines that stood all twisted, windswept, and gnarled. Patches of snow, sometimes three feet deep, occasionally obscured the trail. Agassiz Peak, named after the Swiss glaciologist whose theories inspired young John Muir to develop his own theories of Yosemite, rose high above us, but from this elevation it appeared more as a high hump than as a foreboding Himalayan peak. A symphony of white-crowned sparrows and hermit thrushes piped from the valleys below.

Willy was the first to make it to the lip of the volcanic crater. From down below it looked like he was doing a kachina spirits dance. Mark was next, and then I came trudging along to a spot where I could see out into the desert toward the three Hopi mesas in direct path of the clouds. Erna Fergusson described the climax of the kachina spirits dance at Walpi:

> Finally the priests signaled for the end, sprinkled meal to indicate the line of march, and led their troupe to the second plaza. There the figures were repeated in front of the Snake Rock, where for this occasion a small spruce tree had been planted and decorated with a few floating breath feathers. The priests, as they scattered meal upon the dancers, threw pinches of it also at the tree. The dance was the same. A few more spectators had gathered. A woman, following the priests, quietly threw meal on all the dancers, especially upon the kneeling women figures, whose wigs were becoming well powdered with it. Then the whole party moved to the western plaza.

Their dance was over. But our dance was just beginning. Willy continued on to a higher knob, hopping around with camera in hand. Mark and I scampered around a lesser San Francisco Peak below Humphreys that was layered with deep snow. It was not quite as high as sacred Agassiz but was higher than Fremont Peak. Because there was so much snow, we could not see a species of groundsel called Senecio franciscanus, a yellow flowered tundra plant found nowhere else in the world. To our east stretched the Inner Basin (caused by the sideways explosion two million years ago), with cascades of avalanched snow tumbled on top of older snow, reminiscent of riptide patterns of the New Jersey shore not far from my daughter's place in Hoboken. Tired though we were, we hopped from rock to rock to gain a different perspective. The forests and springs of the Inner Basin looked as inviting as Shangri-la. Light green aspen leaves blended with darker pine and spruce just below the snow line. It was easy to see how this mountain could generate its own weather to send rain clouds eastward.

"Well, whatya think we should say or do up here on this sacred mountain?" Mark inquired of Willy and me as we ate oranges and trail mix.

"Let's just say a wee prayer for a good corn rain," I suggested. We three remained silent for a moment or two. The air up here was supercharged with energy, and although our bodies were weary, we remained just as alert, alive, and excited as we had been at the bottom of the mountain.

Since the hour of 3:00 P.M. rapidly approached and we had lots of snow to negotiate, it was time for us to dance downward through deep snowbanks. But we never left that peak in a sense. Part of our spirits remains up there being infinitely energized.

Sixteen Years Later

An opportunity came sixteen years later to climb Humphreys Peak, the actual highest point in the four-corner state of Arizona. The skies remained just a bit cloudy in a cool northern Arizona. The day before, we arrived in a much hotter Page, Arizona, where I gave a presentation at the Powell Museum on John Wesley Powell's ascent of Longs Peak, Colorado, in 1868, one year prior to his exploration of the Colorado River in cedar boats. Today we would climb Humphreys Peak rising 12,633 feet above sea level. It was now well over a dozen years since our wintry ascent of the San Francisco Peaks in waist-deep snow when we struggled to get within 300 vertical feet of the high point. But on this day, a few days short of my seventy-first birthday, I and my friends Jim Ledbetter and John Sullivan, still in their fifties, remained confident that we would summit Humphreys Peak. We shouldered our camel packs filled with water and sandwiches and energy snacks and began our ascent through a meadow of purple lupines and black-eyed Susans blowing in the wind. The dark pyramid of Humphreys rose above by some 3,000 feet—we knew we were in for a long day.

As we entered a sweet-smelling pine forest, we couldn't help but notice dozens of dark-brown mushrooms springing forth along the trail. Plant communities of white columbines and penstemon grew in profusion. We heard both the screeching of a chickaree squirrel and the jackhammering of a sapsucker in the branches above. It was at this point that the trail began to twist upward with numerous switchbacks helping us gain elevation and broad-sweeping views of volcanic terrain in the distance. As the trail grew steeper, we hopped over exposed spruce roots and lumpy rocks until we at last gained the saddle not far from where we stood in deep snow years ago. We looked across at Agassiz Peak that is closed to climbers to allow for sacred ceremonial plume planting by Hopi runners whose hope it is that this sacred ceremony would foster a fruitful crop of corn. Corn is the true gift of the rain-bearing kachina spirits who dwell in the San Francisco Peaks.

We could see that there were at least three or four false summits that must be gained before the final push up Humphreys Peak. I followed slowly after my younger companions, so slowly that one of them went ahead to reach the summit. He greeted the two of us on his way back! Somehow I lost my balance and jammed my left boot down on a rather hard and pointy piece of black lava, bruising the arch of my foot. I just had to stop to get control of the pain. Would I be able to summit? I stood only a few hundred feet shy of that high peak up in the sky. I thought to myself that I climbed this mountain just after spending four weeks at sea level back East. But no way would I turn around! I hobbled slowly to the top and high-fived it with my friend who was just a little bit ahead of me. In pain still, I took in the vista of the North Rim of the Grand Canyon a hundred miles away and the great desert lands of the Hopi to the northeast. Not at all hungry, I succeeded in forcing down half a sandwich and long swallows of cool water. Clouds built up but with no thunder, thankfully.

We began our slow, very slow descent. Our friend was somewhere far below taking photographs. Jim's knee began to bother him and we wounded ones hobbled at times and carefully sat down to go through rather steep crevices on the seats of our pants. This process continued seemingly without end until we reached the forests and meadows of the valleys below. John said to me back at the car, "I hope Jim and I will be able to do this when we're seventy-one like you!" which made me feel good. Our return trip brought us to the North

Rim of the Grand Canyon where we gazed in wonderment at ever-so distant Humphreys Peak through binoculars. I suppose the tourists around us wondered why we were so fixated on some distant mountain.

IV—Wheeler

For a reprieve from graduate studies at the University of New Mexico, my wife, Maura, and I used to visit the Taos Pueblo nestled beneath snowy Mount Wheeler. One time, we struck up a conversation with a tribal elder who was a member of the tribal council. He said, "Will you look up there at old Mount Wheeler? It's sure sticking up there against the blue sky, isn't it?" When I asked him if he had ever climbed Wheeler, the highest peak in New Mexico, he said that he had done so many times. "Way up there," he said with a chuckle, "there's a spring that remains so cold in the middle of summer that it almost hurts you to drink from it. But I always stop there for a drink." He suggested that we climb it once summer returned. I didn't get around to climbing Mount Wheeler until some thirty years later in the year 2000.

My friend Jonny Boucher, with whom I had climbed Mount Katahdin, Maine, and Halla San, South Korea, came across from England for a short stay in early September. We had decided to climb this mountain despite stern warnings from a dignified, gray-haired British lady, his neighbor, that he surely must realize that this Mount Wheeler stood in the midst of a forbidding desert! We brought along with us my little blond cocker spaniel Mini, who had ascended three fourteeners and eight other thirteeners with me in times past. Although she was born in Summerville, South Carolina, she took to the Colorado tundra like salmon to the Copper River. In Denver, Jonny and I checked trail maps of the Kit Carson National Forest and Mount Wheeler while Mini ate some dog-bone treats. We packed the car that night with camping and climbing supplies and turned in early.

Arriving at a Rio Hondo campsite near Taos Ski Area, we set up our tents, fed Mini, and ate fire-cooked steaks and potatoes. We then proceeded to the trailhead for a twilight glimpse of our climb the next morning. Mini wanted to climb the mountain right then and there. It proved to be an extremely chilly night for early September, and when Mini whimpered in the middle of the night, I opened up my sleeping bag so she could crawl in for extra warmth. Once, in the middle of the night, she got up and crawled in with Jonny, who was simply delighted.

At dawn, we three hopped out of the tent and into the even colder air, our breaths all steaming. Fire lit, we felt a bit warmer, and after we swilled hot coffee, we felt even better. As Mini danced around the fire with an occasional bark for a scrap of food, we stuffed our day packs with energy bars and water and soon hit the trail. Mini, of course, led the way up through Douglas fir and lodgepole pines. Clusters of pink fireweed and pearly everlasting graced the edge of the woods. The trail became steep as we arrived at a small, stagnant pond, where the trail headed due south up a rocky escarpment that afforded us views of the Pecos Mountains and Taos Valley. We rested to chug some water and spritz water into Mini's mouth. She wolfed down a cheddar-cheese cracker and raced ahead on the ever-upward trail. The sky remained azure blue, and by now the sun warmed things up quite a bit. Rugged hills to the southwest still loomed much higher than our elevation of around 10,000 feet.

Jonny and I reminisced about our climbs of the past in Maine, Korea, and only two years earlier, Mount Princeton, just to the north of Tabeguache Peak. For forty-two years, on and off, we had gotten together for a bit of mountaineering. Jonny's highest ascent was Mount Kilimanjaro, well over 19,400 feet. With a guide, it took him four days. Today's ascent would get us to the highest point in the four-corner state of New Mexico at 13,161 feet—slightly less than his ascent of Mount Kinabalu of 13,454 feet in Borneo, when he climbed from warm rain-forest jungles to downright chilly dwarf forests and frosty, damp tundra high above the South China Sea. Jonny had spent more than thirty years of his life in Asia as a bank officer for the Bank of Hong Kong-Shanghai and had devoted his spare time to climbing hills and mountains. But now, much later in our lives, we had a hard time keeping up with pace-setting Mini. She had a way of beckoning you onward with her sad brown eyes and wiggling stump of a tail.

At last we reached tree line and the beginning of a long hump of tundra. We could no longer spot the pronounced heights of Mount Wheeler, as we were able to do far below. Mini chased song sparrows up and down the bald hills, moving her little feet as quickly as the harpsichord notes of a Domenico Scarlatti sonata. She climbed the mountain thrice for our once. Her brown eyes sparkled with joy. Up here, sunflowers blew in breezes in an already browning tundra. Those high peaks to the southwest, including Jicarita Peak, no longer rose above us—they only equaled our elevation. Oh no, our trail began to descend! What's going on here? Should we freelance it over to a false summit to our south? To play it safe, we dutifully descended the switchbacks down into a krummholz forest of limber pines that hissed in the wind. Here we sat down and ate some energy bars that we shared with Mini, who then drank from a stream while we guzzled water from our bottles.

The sky remained clear as we stood up and commenced our hike through twisted pines of tree line straight up into the tundra. The trail showed no mercy as it led us up a fifty-degree slope toward an amazingly level bald ridge. We sixty-plus-year-olds huffed and puffed and rested while Mini dashed skyward like a ballerina doing pirouettes, only to bound back downslope to two human tortoises. She tried to speed us up, to no avail. But we finally stood atop a level ridge that led toward several false summits, with the rocky hump of Wheeler rising even higher. Below us lay the sacred Blue Lake of the Taos Pueblo, glistening like a jewel. It is here that certain secret ceremonial practices have been conducted by this tribe for centuries. President Richard Nixon, in a surprise move, returned the Blue Lake to the Taos Pueblo midway through his first term. It should have never been severed from the Taos Pueblo to begin with. But there it lay, about 500 feet below us, crescent-shaped and nestled against the Mount Wheeler complex. We did see several human figures seated along its shoreline; they were wrapped in colorful blankets.

Just before we started our climb of a false summit, I had shooting pains in my stomach. I had to rest. Poor Jonny thought he had come all the way from London, only to be stopped 300 vertical feet shy of our objective. But miraculously, my pain vanished and we proceeded slowly and cautiously up Mount Walter, a kind of false summit lower than Wheeler. You guessed it—Mini stood atop that peak ten minutes or so before we trudged up to her level. Up here, slightly above 13,000 feet, there was no vegetation to speak of, only gleaming stones. We dropped back down to climb yet another summit with Wheeler rising just a bit higher. Those distant peaks to the southwest clearly lay at a significantly lower elevation. Our campsite valley looked impossibly far away, and in the distance, the table mesa of Taos and vast deserts stretched westward. We could see wee specks of people atop Wheeler perhaps several hundred yards away.

Mini, with her long, flopping ears blowing in the wind, led the way to the summit, where several other dogs, much larger than Mini, accompanied their masters. We gazed all around a great circle of New Mexico lying far below. The air was so clear we could see as far as the Arizona border, with Grandmother Spider Mountain in between. We three sat down for a much needed rest. We drank water and nibbled on cheddar-cheese crackers (which Mini loved) and dried apricots. Very sadly, within a week of our descent from this lofty summit and return trip to Denver, poor Mini died suddenly of autoimmune disease. Her ashes rest in our backyard under a marker on South York Street. I truly loved her as a special spirit of God's creation. For a South Carolina swamp dog, she took to the mountains like no other dog I have known. Jonny e-mailed me from London to share his grief. He called her a priceless little duchess of South York.

10

A WINDY ASCENT OF GUADALUPE PEAK, TEXAS

AFTER LEAVING A COLD and windy Denver to fly to a supposedly much warmer West Texas, we became concerned looking out the aircraft window over southern New Mexico, to see landscapes blanketed with deeply rippled March snow. Surely Texas would be warmer where we would climb Guadalupe Peak rising to the highest point in Texas at 8,749 feet. But, as we approached El Paso International Airport, we noticed white and glistening snow on the north-facing sides of otherwise bare mountains. However, El Paso itself basked in a warm sun with a temperature hovering in the midsixties, some thirty degrees warmer than Denver. Perhaps our plans of climbing this high and windy peak on the New Mexican border would prove to be a bit trickier than we had anticipated.

John Sullivan and I drove our rental car filled with light camping gear eastward for eighty miles or so to Guadalupe Mountains National Park (established in 1972). As we came up to a great white stretch of land, we wondered why there would be snow this far south at a mere 3,000-foot elevation. But our fears vanished when we realized this whiteness proved to be a vast salt flat, the remains of a prehistoric seabed. Gradually El Capitan of the Guadalupe Range took shape with its immense limestone cliffs. We stopped to take photographs of El Capitan framed with a bright green soaptree yucca. Far above rose triangular Guadalupe Peak itself. The terrain ahead of us appeared to be snow-free. Just maybe we would make our climb.

When we arrived at Pine Springs campground, we saw no tent campers, only house trailers. I checked with the campground host to see if it would be all right to set up our tents for the night, but he informed us that unless we had winter gear, we should not try camping. Why? Because it would drop down to the midteens or lower that night. Inasmuch as we wished to get a good night's sleep before climbing another 3,000 feet to the summit from the campground, we elected to rent inexpensive cabins in a nearby town across the New Mexican border. Arising early the next morning, we wolfed down some breakfast bars and quickly swallowed some hot coffee and arrived at the campground at 8:30 A.M. By now, the sun had warmed up the trailhead area to fifty degrees or so, and we wondered just why we had not camped there last night. But telltale signs of heavy frost lurked in the shadows. Guadalupe Peak remained hidden behind a closer limestone ridge and a distant false summit.

We shouldered our camel packs filled with water, snacks, skull caps, and sweaters should they come in handy. Ambling upward past madrone (pronounced MA-drun) trees with bright red trunks, we listened all the while to the shrill notes of a canyon wren. Switching back and forth along the trail toward a higher sandstone cliff, we noticed that the cliff oozed with blackish-red desert varnish caused by leaching iron oxides. Below us spread mesquite bushes and junipers. Prickly pear cactus gleamed in the sun like desert candles and sharp and podded yucca punctuated the mountainside. Guadalupe Peak remained hidden from our view. The higher we climbed, the chillier the air temperature. Approaching the top of a higher limestone ridge, we spotted a girl putting on a sweater as her hair streamed out in the wind. By the time we reached her, sharp gusts blew through the branches of pinyon pines lending a needled, hissing voice to the wind. No wonder the girl added on a heavy sweater. We spoke with her briefly to discover she hailed from Bavaria and was intent on climbing a summit so different from the wetter, densely vegetated Bavarian Alps. As she left us, she bade farewell, and we slipped on sweaters, zipped up our jackets, and donned skull caps. We sort of staggered along the windy trail laced with ankle-deep snow perhaps a few hundred yards behind her. A sudden gust of wind almost flattened me, and as I struggled to stand up straight, a young man scantily clad passed by us saying that strong winds forced him to turn around. Years ago a Shoshone elder named Rupert Weeks had prophesied that a great wind would howl across all of North America for one year. Had it started now? I no longer felt sure that we could make it; besides my tired bones would turn seventy years old in a few months. But younger John pointed to the ascending trail that entered woodlands where we would be protected from the wind. True enough, after a few hundred yards farther, the fierce wind abated as we entered the cover of a sweet-smelling pinyon-juniper forest.

I felt reassured until I spotted fresh mountain lion tracks with deep claw prints! John reminded me that we had two stout walking sticks each for defense. Within a quarter mile or so, there were no longer any lion tracks and no bright yellow eyes lurked above us, at least none that we could see. But I still felt nervous. A mountain lion sees you at least one hour before you see it! Ahead of us lay an unusually lush meadow at a thirty-degree angle beneath a false summit a little over halfway of the four-mile trail to the summit. Sparrows fluttered among deep blue-green agave plants (the source of tequila) and green lechuguilla spines and very large Spanish bayonets, all gleaming in a bright sun under Texas-blue skies, all looking like a Paul Cezanne painting. A distant coyote yelp echoed in the valleys below. At last we reached the top of the false summit to gain a great view of Guadalupe Peak rising still higher like a Mayan pyramid. Our trail ascended the lee side of the peak out of the gusty winds, but for now, we had to descend into a ravine between the peaks and cross a bridge built over a very steep gap. Shortly thereafter, we resumed our ascent of 800 vertical feet to the summit rising far above distant El Capitan.

Somewhere just shy of the summit, we peered out at the vast salt flats 5,000 feet lower and each gust of wind brought the taste of ancient sea salts to our lips. We paused for some water and trail snacks to revive our energy and spirits. All we had left to climb were several thick layers of crumbly limestone so typical of the Guadalupe Mountains. Melting snow seeps through this honey-combed limestone to form a series of caves deep underneath. The much larger caves of Lechuguilla and Carlsbad across the New Mexican border are the results of leaching limestone over millions of years. Carlsbad Caverns has ceilings within it approaching 300 feet high with dripping limestone stalactites. But all these caves lay deep beneath our feet. What concerned us was getting to the actual summit of the peak. John raced ahead of me to photograph a full 360-degree sweep and meet up with the Bavarian girl who sat huddled in the rocks as she ate her lunch in the fiercely gusting winds.

Five minutes later, I arrived at the top that is marked with an aluminum triangle six feet high, and joined in a three-way conversation, or should I say shouting match, in irregular gusts of wind with a temperature in the low forties. Who knows what the windchill figure was? I asked the German girl what interested her the most about America. To my delight she responded "American literature, particularly Native American literature." Did I have any suggestions for her reading? I named some novels of leading Native American writers including those of N. Scott Momaday, Louise Erdrich, Leslie Marmon Silko, and James Welch. She wanted to know what themes she should be looking for. "A connection with the land," I shouted in a constant and forceful wind. We three mused on the fact that we could not help but have a strong connection with the land so high above Texas, especially with the taste of prehistoric salt on our lips. Climbing Guadalupe Peak, way above a salty desert, is a great place to experience the essence of becoming and being a part of Nature.

11

SAND DUNES OF THE HIGH DESERT

I—Great Sand Dunes

THROUGHOUT THE YEARS, these dunes have always magnetically allured me as a kind of spiritual home. I never quite figured out why, until this visit, they, of all places, satisfy my inner being so much. I've flown over them at 30,000 feet to see all thirty-six square miles of them at once, camped by them in cold and blustery sleet, and ambled to the top of them with my family in ninety-degree heat. But this time during cool, dry, windy weather, I've come to understand them in ways unknown to me before. It is not just their size—more than 700 feet high—that makes them "great."

At five o'clock in the evening late in May, I caught my tenth glimpse (but first solo) of the Great Sand Dunes of southern Colorado looking like a giant brain beneath the snowy Sangre de Cristo Mountains. My head ached after a long drive from Laramie, Wyoming, in heavy interstate traffic through Denver, and I was weary (in the late 1980s) of a year's worth of seemingly nonstop teaching at the university. But I just had to ramble out onto the dunes and wade through an ice-cold, pulsing Medano Creek made up of sand and melting snow. One of the pulses (created by sand rhythmically letting loose of all it can momentarily absorb) almost knocked me over before I regained my balance. My sharp headache vanished like a pile of wind-dispersed sand. The wind gusted to thirty miles per hour and blew stinging, multicolored particles of sand against my skin. That million-year-old volcanic debris from the San Juan Mountains across the San Luis Valley felt good stinging my face and hands and gritting the enamel of my teeth. Advancing beyond receding waters of the pulsing stream, I left tracks in the welted, wet sand. But already dry wisps of sand blew out across the wetter sand to change quickly and create dry sands before my very eyes. From there on, I had the dunes to myself and proceeded through strands of Indian rice grass up into the dry tan mounds rising hundreds of feet above my head. The strong sun shining from a turquoise-blue sky felt good.

I followed a narrow ridge at the crest of a dune angling upward at thirty degrees. Sand blew over the edge of the crest suspending my shadow in midair as though I were but a shimmering ghost. At the very crest, the sand seemed firmer than to the windward side where softer piles of fresh sand formed, continually re-creating the actions of Proteus, Greek god of metamorphosis. Henry David Thoreau wrote in his essay "Natural History of Massachusetts" that "Nature is mythical and mystical always, and works with license and extravagance of genius." The Great Sand Dunes are living testimony to Nature's extravagance of genius. Deep dark pits below me, seen through a veil of windblown sand, seemed to be of another world. As I hoofed along the crest, unbelievably jagged and snowy spires of Crestone Peak gradually grew in height as I inched higher and higher into the sky until I could see miles on end of spreading sands in this little piece of Arabia in Colorado. All of the tensions of work and car travel completely evaporated as I stood and stared.

Back at camp, after an exhilarating run downslope and splashing through icy waters, I cooked a modest meal of rice and beans and leafed through a paperback volume of Ralph Waldo Emerson that I had brought along with me.

He confirmed my beliefs about our human relationship to the land in his poem "Hamatreya" in which the spirit of Earth says,

> They called me theirs,
> Who so controlled me,
> Yet every one
> Wished to stay, and is gone,
> How am I theirs,
> If they cannot hold me,
> But I hold them?

This very high set of one-million-year-old dunes that spreads over thirty-six square miles of Earth cannot and will not be held by us except in our minds and spirits.

I looked up from Emerson to see a sky of golden fire setting over the dunes darkening in layers of deep shadow. Wafts of sweet-scented narrow-leaf cottonwoods filtered the air as robins started their evening chorus. With a bright moon rising over Sierra Blanca Peak, I walked leisurely out toward the head of the dunes past sweet sage and ghostly ring muhly grasses that actually grow in circles to trap sparse desert rains. Out of the corner of my eyes, I caught sight of a large cluster of distant phantom pinyon pines engulfed in encroaching sands under darkening skies. I walked up to them and examined their root-like branches at ground level and the tips of buried branches. Park geologists have measured these advancing sands and determined that they are moving into the forest at a rate of seventeen feet per year! As these trees become buried, they form new mounds upon which future living sands build. John Muir believed that seeming natural destruction is but an act of creation, even something so violent, or as he wrote, "joyous," as an earthquake or erupting volcano.

Back at camp, I lit a fire with purchased juniper wood under the brightening stars of the Big Dipper and other constellations. Plumes of sweet-smelling smoke rose to the heavens above. Edward Abbey writes in *Desert Solitaire* that juniper smoke evokes all of the magic and power of the American West. This smoke was my incense burning in the temple of the sand dunes. I got out my bedroll, found a soft spot in the sandy soil, and crawled in to stargaze. A bright star rose over the dunes, while the moon hid behind creaking pine branches as though it were some kind of emerging blossom. The Big Dipper floated directly overhead. Only desert breezes and the gurgling stream broke an intense silence. Silver threads of clouds illuminated by the moon formed part of my dream world until morning when the dunes turned red as the sun ever so gradually peeked over the Sangre de Cristo Mountains.

It was the shrill whistle of "pearl-dip, pearl-dip," made by a circling hawk, which awakened me. Ten mule deer fed on new pine branches within a few feet of my sleeping bag. A chorus of robins, western meadowlarks, and warblers picked up in tempo as a reddish-golden moon set to the west. The dunes reddened in the rising sun and gradually turned pink until they returned to their daytime tan color. I raised myself up on one elbow to have sand particles flick past my eyes; my eyebrows and hair had become laden with sand much like the phantom pine trees of last evening. As I drank a cup of coffee, my mind began to grasp why these dunes mean so much to me, to my inner spirit. They literally, as well as figuratively, made me become a part of them, much like our experience atop Guadalupe Peak with salt on our lips. As Leslie Silko's character Tayo (in her novel *Ceremony)* says as he speaks to a distant mountain lion up on a ridge, "Mountain lion . . . mountain lion, becoming what you are with each breath, your substance changing with the earth and sky."

The shifting, blowing, glowing, darkening dunes of sand here in southern Colorado do much for the human spirit temporarily locked into a body. Their presence becomes part of your hair and more importantly part of your psychic and spiritual fiber. Perhaps they induce a greater self-awareness. I left the dunes with particles of sand in my hair and even inside Emerson's book.

II—North Park Sand Hills

For years I had always noticed in the distance what looked like sand dunes in the northeastern corner of North Park in northern Colorado. Instead of lying at the base of the Sangre de Cristo Mountains, these smaller dunes rested at the foot of the Rawah Mountains not far from the Wyoming border.

In mid-June my younger daughter Maureen and I decided to investigate. We departed Laramie in a southwesterly direction toward the North Park of Colorado in Jackson County north of the town of Walden.

While Wyoming's Snowy Range appeared dark and stormy, Colorado's distant Rawahs gleamed with brilliant bands of snow, much whiter than lingering clouds above them. They looked like part of a netherworld only momentarily in contact with Earth. As we drove toward the wooded fringes of the southern end of the Laramie Plains, the University of Wyoming's Jelm Mountain Observatory sparkled like a day star on the horizon.

We entered the forest above Woods Landing to catch a glimpse of a solitary mule deer standing at roadside and glancing cautiously at us. We proceeded through angular groves of lodgepole pines lining the roadside interspersed with delicately trembling light-green aspens. Deeper in Fox Park, aspen groves attain considerable height; some of the trees with their white bark reminded me of graceful groves of bamboo trees back in Japan where we had lived a few years before. Forest gave way to fields of open sagebrush beyond the Colorado line, and a few more fringes of lodgepole pines held their own against the edge of a big, dry valley called North Park. One high Egyptian pyramid–shaped hill bulged upward with its north side forested and its south side bald. I pointed southward to the Park Range where winter still lingered.

Breezes bent grasses eastward in the wide expanse of North Park. But where are those sand hills? Almost to Cowdrey, Colorado, we saw them, the tips of them, looming to the east just below the Rawahs. We found a little dirt road that angled eastward in the right direction and took it. We couldn't help but smell the sweet grass growing along the shoreline of a pond. No wonder the Cheyenne Indians make use of sweet grass for sacred incense. Glad to park our car several miles in, we got out and walked briskly over to sandy hills dotted with sagebrush. Black angus cattle munched on tall stalks of grass beneath the distant Never Summer Mountains blanketed with snow. We ambled along toward aspen-fringed ridges just ahead of the sand dunes themselves.

It was relaxing to walk cross-country past clusters of flowers bobbing in the wind. Every so often we glanced at the high Park Range rising to the west. We sensed its presence even after we looked away from the range. About an hour's hike took us to the first several miles of sandy hills interspersed with patches of aspen, white pine, and sagebrush. Once out in the open, we saw scores of animal tracks in the sand including cloven hoof prints of antelope. The tracks made the pulverized sand glisten all the more. We couldn't help but notice many different colored minerals on the sides of forty-foot-high sand dunes. We had found them at last!

Jay Roberts of the Wyoming State Geological Survey was kind enough to analyze a sand sample that I brought back to Laramie. Here is the result of his analysis: quartz (75.8 percent), plagioclase (17.2 percent), amphibole (4.0 percent), potassium feldspar (2.8 percent), magnetite (0.3 percent), and just a trace of sphene (titanium ore). All of these minerals are of igneous or meta-morphic origin. Like the Great Sand Dunes, these much smaller dunes have formed on the easterly edge of a broad, dry valley surrounded by high mountains eroding their surfaces to the prevailing winds. And, as with the Great Sand Dunes, constant winds push the sand as far eastward as they can to the base of the mountains, sometimes at the expense of trees swallowed alive by mounting sand. Maureen and I noticed that some aspen trees at the northeast edge of the dunes attempted to grow faster than the advancing sands. Hopefully they will survive.

But unlike a trapped tree, my daughter romped up and down the dunes—some over forty feet high, feeling complete joy and giggling as she slid downslope just as she had done with her sister, Michelle, and brother, Rich, at the Great Sand Dunes so many times. After a half hour or so, we both continued our exploration of the vegetation trying to fight back the sand's advance. Juniper shrubs, kinnikinnick (a native tobacco used by Native Americans), rabbitbrush, and shrubby cinquefoil all shared in resisting the advance of sand.

The sky grew darker and we had to leave this magical place in advance of a storm that began to thrash the Park Range with lightning. Marsh hawks hovered in air currents between mountain and storm. Our minds had truly been ionized by the rare energies of these sand hills. Such sandy rambles are surely needed every now and then.

12

CLIMBING HIGH IN THE PECOS AND SAN JUAN MOUNTAINS

I—Jicarita

THEY BECKON ALL who gaze at their glistening banks of snow above blue-green skirts of forest. South Truchas Peak is New Mexico's third highest, at 13,102 feet. It dominates the Pecos Wilderness Area and the minds of people who come under its spell. These mountains have certainly engendered numerous mythic stories. One of them concerns greedy Spaniards in search of gold. A young Indian lad called Pin-ne-qua, who was susceptible to flattery, led forty Spaniards into the high mountains, where he had earlier stumbled across a vein of gold. Kiosh, the evil one who remains strong in the hearts of those who seek material wealth, immediately entered upon the scene. He changed the course of the sun, causing the gold seekers to trudge in the wrong direction. A thirst-crazed Spaniard killed Pin-ne-qua in a rage. Eventually, each and every thirsty soldier dropped to his death.

Not seeking gold and having plenty of water, Mark Reames and I packed into the Pecos Wilderness from the Santa Barbara Campground, where glittering evening stars had entranced us the night before. Now, pines glowed resinously in the morning sun. Forty shades of green raced up the mountainsides in the form of aspen, dwarf maple, squaw current, and numerous other varieties of underbrush. Bursts of color punctuated the inclining trail: lavender shooting stars, blue-and-white columbines, purple iris, scarlet Indian paintbrush, sulphur flower, and clusters of golden banner. Perhaps Pin-ne-qua's vein of gold was really nothing more or less than golden banner. Imagine armor-plated Spaniards marching in columns to seize golden banner!

We sat for a rest in the depths of an aspen grove, serenaded by the ethereal notes of a Swainson's thrush, much like some distant Indian flute player. For us, the thrush matched the landscape, translating it with rare refinement. Its notes enter the spirit's core. Our backpacks became more burdensome the higher we hiked. With this pack, I weighed more than 220 pounds and trudged much like an overly heavy man placing one foot firmly ahead and gliding the body forward as though walking were an engineering project. We took many rests. We took many swigs of water, thankful we were not Spanish soldiers, as thirsty as dogs, being led by Pin-ne-qua. At times, the trail up the Middle Fork skirted the edge of the slope like a mountain goat's path. When we arrived at a gently sloping meadow of skunk cabbage and tall grasses, we dispensed of our packs to scout out a campsite. Finding one by a trickling brook in a cathedral of tall white aspen, we set up camp with a ring of rocks for a fire and fallen logs for seats.

To the southwest rose the Barbara Divide, flanked with snow. Behind us, a densely forested slope of aspen, fir, and spruce rising up to the obscured Jicarita Peak. The roar of the Middle Fork River far below resonated pleasingly through the forest and meadow. I filled and purified a jug of water for cooking our meal and lit a campfire in the late afternoon sun. Thankfully we had sufficient water and juice to quench our thirst.

As the sun sank below a western ridge, a bright crescent moon with its partner Jupiter appeared, and then the Big Dipper and Mars. Before long, the Way of Souls, or the Milky Way, glittered like a ceremonial sash across the sky. Ralph Waldo Emerson once wrote that if the stars had appeared but once in human history, it would have been recorded in memory as a phenomenal, mythological event worthy of worship. Shooting stars dashed across the sky like tracer bullets. The temperature on this late June night started to drop, forcing us back to the fire and into our sleeping bags to watch the stars flicker and gleam until they became part of our dreams.

We awakened at 6:15 A.M. to a glorious, cloudless morning. Again, I lit a fire to kill the frost that had gathered around our campsite vegetation. Amazing to think meadow flowers could withstand such a burden each night! But they adjust somehow, just like humans adjust to the burdens of heavy backpacks. Skies of stars and skies of sun help nurture these flowers to fullness of bloom.

After breakfast, we put hard-boiled eggs, candy bars, oranges, and cheese into our day packs and made sure our canteens were filled to the brim. Our destination? Jicarita Peak, looming in the sky at 12,750 feet, flanked with deep snow on its eastern side. Notes from Swainson's thrushes and ruby-crowned kinglets lifted our spirits as we walked ever higher on the trail. The more elevation we gained, the smaller and less mature grew the skunk cabbage in even chillier air. We paused to listen to the high-pitched shrill of the whistle pig that scurried along the rocky exposures beneath the tundra. Why were there outcroppings of rock flows every now and then? Were they encouraged by destabilizing water seepage and underground springs? Rock flows streaked the mountain like strokes of gray in a Monet painting. Clusters of flag irises lent a pointillistic touch.

A raven cawed, refocusing our attention to alpine heights forever above in a blue dome of sky. We again quickly paced up through the tree line into bald tundra. The usual pipits and rosy finches flicked through the air, warmed by the burning disk of radium in the sky. Still there were no clouds. Within an hour we stood, at last, atop the Santa Barbara Divide to stare into New Mexican space far and near. Near our feet grew delicate pink Parry's primrose, white moss campion, and purple alpine forget-me-nots. Far away spread hazy depressions of Mora Valley and the flat desert of the eastern plains. A stiff alpine breeze grew even stronger, so we dropped below a protective ledge and snacked on our lunch of sky for the soul and food for the body. The sky defines western lands like no other region in America. Western clouds sometimes even replicate terraced landforms below, as though the land had urged the clouds into conformity. Nowhere else have I sensed planetary space stretching forever as I have here in the great American West. The sky does indeed feed the soul. We know we are part of the universe. It's as though we stood on some fresh and new planet that was light-years away.

We moved on toward the summit of Jicarita Peak along a faint trail lined with blue sky pilots and yellow alpine avens. Skirting the flanks of an adjoining peak, we scrambled upward to the windiest spot in New Mexico—or so it seemed. Others thought so, anyway, as a high windbreak of rocks had been constructed to give climbers a reprieve. Now that we stood at the very summit, it was time to explore. And we ambled across to its Taos side and gazed at New Mexico's highest peak, Mount Wheeler, and at the ever-so-distant Wolf Creek Pass and the San Juan Range of southern Colorado, which we would explore in another season. All of the San Juan peaks lay socked in snow and impossible to climb without winter gear and stern determination. Sunny Jicarita was a good choice indeed for today, despite the wind, but it was good not just for panoramic views. Along came some bighorn sheep. They nudged closer and closer toward us, looking a bit like helmeted conquistadors. They came ridiculously close. Now we could see their soft brown eyes and the gray ridges of their curved horns. They reared up on their hind legs, pretending to challenge each other. I backed away, although Mark seemed less shy than I was. Clearly we had invaded their territory, and they simply moved us off the peak, herding us like sheep. We rapidly descended an angular snowfield while they stood holding their ground as kings of the mountain. We had come eyeball to eyeball with creatures that are much closer to the land than we are.

After another snack at the base of the snowfield, we waved good-bye to our brief acquaintances, who were still guarding the mountaintop and descended quickly to tree line filled with thrush and kinglet music. We soon returned to our peaceful campsite. Another fire lit, we wolfed down hot stew and watched the sun sink into the western desert. The atmosphere glowed as golden as Spanish dreams. From stargazing to sleep to the next morning's light seemed like mere minutes in a bubble of time.

I sipped with pleasure from my steaming mug of coffee as I stood amid very frosty flowers. This third day in the backcountry of New Mexico proved to be cloudless, although a distant forest fire haze had become visible to the west. Today we would go up a different draw to the Barbara Divide, closer to the snowy Truchas (Trout) Peaks. Lunches in our packs, we crossed the Middle Fork Rapids on two shaky logs, one being slicker than grease. We then sprang up the trail lined with mossy spruce and entered an open meadow graced with a gentle stream that cut into banks with swirling pools—ideal for brook trout. Pin-ne-qua and his Spaniards should have come to these golden, well-watered meadows. No sign of Kiosh, the evil one—just butterflies and robins and endless bright flowers under a blue arch of sky.

Our trail became somewhat steep and we soon saw our first patch of snow. Before long, the snow wasn't in patches but in one continuous field, which deepened the higher we trudged. A foolish time for me to be in short pants! Sometimes I'd fall through the snow and scratch my legs on poking branches on the way down. It wasn't much fun getting back out. At times my scratches created their own watermelon snow—snow with a pink tinge. I was sorely tempted to head over to a soggy marsh laced with marsh marigolds and take my chances with mud rather than snow, but I could see clear tundra a few hundred yards ahead. A little higher up, the more hardened snow gave us a bit of support. We were thankful to step out onto the sunny, clear tundra under the turquoise heavens above. Sky thoughts prevailed. Isolated though the tundra is, loneliness is hardly a factor—too many sky pilots and alpine forget-me-nots.

Atop the divide we peered into space—hundreds of miles of space. To our west loomed the Truchas Peaks, which stood well over 13,000 feet and remained as white as Moby Dick. To our east stretched the foothills and distant summit of Hermit Peak above Las Vegas, New Mexico. To our north rose yesterday's mountain guarded by bighorn rams. To our south, we saw the dim outline of Sandia Crest hugging the outskirts of Albuquerque. Sandia Mountain's western face appears at sunset to be like a giant, split-open watermelon—hence its Spanish name. Again memories came to mind of my attempted climb of Sandia in February when what I thought was a talcum powder dusting of snow turned out to be waist-deep. Here on the Barbara Divide, tiny stones sparkled at my feet. Upon closer examination, I discovered not gold but quartzite arrow chippings from Pin-ne-qua's people, the ancient Pueblos. They, like the Spanish, must have enjoyed their mutton as these mountaintops are fairly well sprinkled with quartzite points. A few of the arrows were made of dark obsidian, probably obtained through trade with the tribes of Mexico.

Descending, we avoided the deep snow and took our chances with wet marshes, which led to lower, drier vales. Wet and soggy they were but equally flowerful with white marsh marigolds and yellow snow buttercups. Thrushes serenaded us. Distant waterfalls thundered. But we really had to find the trail once again. It meant climbing up through shallower snow all the while looking for footprints. Where were our footprints? What if we crossed our old trail on slightly open ground where there were no prints? What if . . . and there they were—sets of melting holes in a foot of snow. A mile of this down-hilling got us to scant patches and eventually the open, dusty trail.

It was good to bathe in a meadow stream below. The sun was strong enough to counteract the icy water gathered into a moderately deep pool. Butterflies fluttered and all the feathered gang sang. We would watch stars that evening in the peace and security of our campsite where we caught the stronger scent of that distant forest fire. Once the hazy sun had risen the next morning, going back down with lighter packs to civilization was all we had left to do. We had seized several days of our lives from the city to be in the peaks of the Pecos near and far.

II—Sneffels

Dawn's first glimmer revealed the silver tones of subalpine firs. High peaks, looming above the Blue Lakes, began to glow like fragments of the moon brought closer to Earth. Today we would climb a twenty-six-million-year-old volcanic spire known as Mount Sneffels in the San Juan Mountains of south-western Colorado. There are two other Sneffels (spelled slightly differently) on our planet; one caps the top of the Isle of Man in the Irish Sea and the other is an extinct volcanic cone that rises out of a very white glacier in southwestern Iceland. Yesterday we had noticed its north-facing, angular snowfields above Ridgeway, Colorado, but now, as I crawled out of the tent, it appeared naked and barren, yet alluring, so high it rose in an orange sky.

Back in 1874, when Frederic Endlich of the Hayden Expedition first cast his eyes on this jagged spire, he exclaimed, "There's Snaefell," referring to a volcanic mountain inside Snaefellsjokull (Snaefells Glacier), Iceland, in Jules Verne's *Journey to the Center of the Earth.* As we plodded along our trail 120 years later than the Hayden Expedition, I had the impression that I was on a journey to the center of the moon—a moon with flowers, that is. Along our way toward the upper Blue Lakes there bloomed a profusion of colorful flowers: ever-so-rosy paintbrush, blue columbine, purple larkspur, yellow alpine avens, red queen's crown, and pink moss campion. All of these soft and delicate plants contrasted with spires of hard rock in the sun. The basin echoed with the high-pitched squeaking of marmots and squawking ravens high in the sky. Now we could see across our lower basin from the top of the rolling tundra slopes, which reminded me of coastal Newfoundland, Canada. They were soft underfoot, just as I remembered from my three-week birding excursion to Newfoundland in 1958. The lower and upper Blue Lakes form a large volcanic caldera that helped furnish sand for the Great Sand Dunes over millions of years. Huge black and brown volcanic spires scratched the blue sky. Soft tundra and volcanic rock marry to form a San Juan haiku of contrasting beauty.

It was peaceful walking along the shoreline of the third Blue Lake. We noted small circles form on the lake's surface, indicating the presence of trout. Our trail suddenly rose with zigzags upward like stitches on the side of a steep, dark ridge, at the top of which rested Blue Lake Pass. My son, Rich, led the way, with Mark Reames and me following. Sometimes the width of the trail occupied only a few inches of steep, angular slope. One false move and you'd be history. Still the flowers grew among pinnacles of rock. All-white columbines graced the interior of one little rocky nook far above the wind-rippled Blue Lakes. At nighttime such flowers are iridescent even without the moon. Starlight is enough to give them a glow. Snowfields add to this effect. That is why, I believe, Frank Waters contends in his book *The Colorado* that the Rockies emit light all of their own in the dark of night.

Who can say how far my mind wandered off this steep and very narrow trail, although my feet remained glued to it. Upward forever. My son and Mark momentarily disappeared—because they stood atop Blue Lakes Pass at 13,000 feet. And then came me. Yankee Boy Basin spread eastward, and then stubborn Mount Sneffels, with all sorts of Mont Blanc-like spires that rose forever above. One climber sat with his daughters sporting a handmade cane that had a curved hickory wood handle. It resembled an ice axe, although it was much lighter and more manageable. Another group of boisterous climbers from Kansas assembled below us, pondering their route up Sneffels from this pass via difficult spires, or back into Yankee Boy Basin and up a steep and rocky couloir. They didn't seem to pay any attention to a sprite-like rosy finch hopping at their feet. Perhaps it had flown down from the summit in a moment's time. My climbing party elected to descend to the beginning of the couloir, but not without sitting and staring westward into a brown-peaked volcanic basin above our campground. We knew we would explore this trailless valley on another day when we hoped to have Sneffels behind us. We wanted to take the time to sit and listen to cascading rocks tumbling from peaks above, to collect a geode or two, to watch buck deer dance across the tundra, and finally to wash our faces late in the day in the icy spray of waterfalls.

But Sneffels had to be ascended before late afternoon thunderheads built up. It is no place to be with thrashing lightning and volcanic thunder. Down we plodded to the very flowerful upper fields of Yankee Boy Basin, where adventuresome men mined silver and gold. One of them must have been a young Yankee from New England. Our gold and silver lay ahead of us in the form of adventure. Our necks hurt as we looked straight up this rocky, dusty couloir with ant-like climbers hundreds of feet above. Step by step is the way—not to worry about how long it will take or how tired you will get as on the San Francisco Peaks. However, my boot tread was badly worn and I slipped backward too often for comfort. As my son and Mark climbed steadily above, I moved over to bigger rocks and things went better. I made time by grabbing one boulder after another until humans below appeared as ants. But there remained half a couloir above with tiny human heads peering over the edge at me and others. A rock from far above came loose and tumbled downhill, clinking and clanking and clacking along the way. French climbers shouted to each other, *"Faites attention, attention!"* They quickly moved out of the way as the rock fell harmlessly to the base without injury to anyone.

With hundreds more hand grabs and wobbly rocks underfoot, I made it to the lip of the couloir, where Mark stood all smiles. Rich had gone up yet another narrow couloir to the summit. I followed Mark closely up a rockier, snowy couloir as Yankee Boy Basin unfolded below like a dream. We could see a big boulder had torn loose, leaving a trail of chink marks and chips on lower rocks and ledges. A half hour later we arrived at the 14,000-foot lip of a narrow chute. Rich stood above us and waved. "This way," he said, as he pointed to a narrow chimney to our left. Up we shimmied and out onto a dirt and stone trail that led us to the top of the 14,150-foot crest of Mount Sneffels. With a third of Colorado spreading below, we stood and stared, barely controlling the grins on our faces atop the highest of surrounding spires in the sun.

Postscript

Just one week later, Mark Reames fell to his death in the mountains above Boulder, Colorado, on a relatively easy scramble across some rocky ledges. He was with his brother on his brother's birthday. The fact that it could have happened on Sneffels haunted both Rich and me for months. I treasure those moments in the sky with Mark. He was a true companion along many a trail.

13

A CLOSE CALL ON MOUNT PRINCETON

I HAD WANTED to climb Mount Princeton (14,197 feet) ever since my late friend Mark Reames suggested ascending this mountain several years ago. I grew up in central New Jersey, where my father served as a reference librarian at Princeton University for nearly twenty years after he had managed Parnassus Bookshop off-campus during and slightly after World War II. Mark was a Yale man who had climbed the higher Mount Yale but never Mount Princeton; he wanted to broaden his Ivy League experience by climbing Princeton and then enjoying a hot soak in Mount Princeton's hot springs just outside Buena Vista, Colorado.

Even after Mark's unexpected and tragic death from a fall in the mountains above Boulder, I still wanted to climb this mountain and arranged to do so with my son, Rich, and friends Jonny Boucher (with whom I climbed Mount Wheeler), Gordon and Walt Fader (with whom I had climbed Wilson Mountain), and Michael Mackey. We attempted to climb Mount Princeton (without Jonny Boucher, who was detained by his mother's illness) in early August 1997.

We woke up at our campsite in chilly air with a steady, light rain and, donning our ponchos, ate our breakfast bars and oranges. We soon trekked up a steep and winding gravel road under slowly brightening clouds. Reaching the tundra around noon, we ate our lunches in the shelter of a small cave that protected us from increasing winds and pelting snow mixed with sleet. Michael Mackey opened a can of sardines for his lunch and succeeded in fuming up the cave as though it were some sort of Viking's cache of aging shark meat on the frigid seacoast of Iceland. We quickly exited the cave and proceeded along the trail with barely fifty feet of visibility. Our ponchos flared out in the wind like giant bat wings. Should we continue? We decided to go around the next bend to see how it looked. Other descending climbers, all covered with a thick layer of snow, warned us not to continue, as hurricane-force winds raged on the upper ridge that led to the pyramid-shaped summit. However, we slogged along the trail for another quarter mile with freezing hands and feet and ponchos almost ripping off our backs. After Walt Fader and I almost slipped off the trail, I finally said we must turn around. All reluctantly agreed. This was my first unsuccessful attempt on a Colorado fourteener. We had made it to an elevation of slightly more than 13,000 feet in this fierce August storm with decreasing visibility. What would we have ever seen from the summit had we managed to get there? Even the visibility back in Denver a day later proved to be incredibly limited, with freak thunderstorms and hailstorms dumping ice pellets so deep that snow-plows were brought out to remove as much as two feet of hail from city streets in early August. I'm sure the summit of Mount Princeton, had we made it, would have seemed like Antarctica in winter.

One year later, almost to the day, my English friend Jonny Boucher arrived in Colorado to climb Mount Princeton shortly after he finished a fifty-mile trek along the Saint James Trail in the Pyrenees. This summer's ascent would mark the fortieth anniversary of our climb with Gordon Fader of Mount Katahdin in northern Maine. We booked a campsite at Mount Princeton's base for four nights straight in case we had to wait for bad weather to abate. That evening, Jonny, myself, and a young French-speaking college student, Herve Picherit, watched rain clouds gather and lightning fork the sky. We felt certain that we would not be able to climb the next day. But several hours before we turned in for the night, the stars came out, along with a thin, Arabic sliver of moon. The narrow valleys filled with gossamer threads of cloud that spread in slow motion to our very own campground, where a crackling log fire snapped with as many sparks as there were stars in the sky. Jonny chatted a good bit about his great Spanish hike along the pilgrim's trail. But now he was very anxious to climb his second Rocky Mountain and the second highest ever—some 5,000 feet lower than icy Kilimanjaro.

The next day dawned clear, with the strong scent of pines freshened by the rain of the day before. As we ate our breakfast bars, pert Canada jays hopped from branch to branch begging for food. We packed our gear and cheerfully drove our four-wheel drive vehicle as far up as tree line just in case we needed to make a rapid retreat. Unthinkingly, I drove up to a higher knoll, not wanting to get blocked in by other cars on a narrow road. I was glad to have that open space slightly above the skinny, winding road, as several other cars followed us. Shouldering our packs, we sprung out onto the tundra, which was covered with thick patches of yellow alpine avens, and deftly handled the first rocky ridge at about 11,800 feet. Another series of ridges loomed above with alpine harebells, chiming bells, and alpine gentians (cousin to arctic gentians that we observed much later in life up in Iceland), all bright blue, lacing the damp ground. Mist rose up from the rain-soaked valleys only to be burnt off by the bright alpine sun. Here we were on the upper approaches to Mount Princeton, a far cry from walking the Princeton University campus in front of Nassau Hall on the way to Firestone Library! Jagged slopes of other collegiate peaks, including Yale and Harvard, rose in the distance. Marmots' squeaks echoed from alpine rills to alpine walls of rock.

We stopped for water and caught our breath. The air of almost 13,000 feet started to get to us, along with the challenge of yards and yards of upsloping loose, wobbly rocks. I paused to rest my legs and enjoy the rare beauty of yellow, orange, and green lichens that abundantly coated the boulders all around us. Alpine thistles swayed on their stalks in between a jumble of rocks. This was a far cry from sitting in the warmth and comfort of my father's 1940s bookshop in Princeton and listening to young poets the likes of W. S. Merwin, Galway Kinnell, and William Meredith. But up here on Mount Princeton we listened to the poetry of the wind and the cheeping of rosy finches.

We climbed yet another false summit to peer out onto alpine heights looming above, and the lower couloir, where we had been forced to turn around in the fierce winds of last year. Squawking ravens circled the skies. At our feet lay two inches of fresh August snow from last night's storm. We paused to eat oranges while sitting on black rocks (Princeton University's two colors) and to rest our wobbly knees. We knew we must summit the final peak no later than noon for fear of afternoon thunderstorms christening us with rain and lightning bolts. Black storm clouds gathered to the west, but thankfully they remained distant. We three huffed and puffed to reach the pointy summit of 14,167 feet, almost 6,000 feet higher than the highest point in windy Texas. We sat under a rock cairn to catch our breath and chat with several other climbers. Silently we celebrated our achievement high above the misty veils of clouds, pierced here and there by imposing peaks. Pikas screeched from the ledges below us, seeming to beckon us to descend.

Our descent route led us over steep, angled, and wobbly rocks gurgling with deep underground streams that reminded both Jonny and me of our descent of Mount Katahdin forty years ago—an underground concert of trickles, drips, and intermittent sounds. Even though Jonny spent the past forty years in banking and I in academe, we had a lot in common, particularly our love of mountains and our love of Asia. Our careful trek down became so steep at times that my toes painfully crammed into the front of my boots. As we passed the Icelandic "fish cave," where we ate lunch a year ago, we reflected that it had been a wise choice back then not to try and reach the summit, as it took us nearly two hours of rapid descent to arrive here *without* blowing snow and howling winds!

We left the trail to cross over to our car, which was perched on its lonesome knoll. I immediately put the car in four-wheel drive, low gear, and tried to ease it down the hill to the winding road below. But neither low gear nor the brakes held nearly as tightly as I had hoped. As we gained speed, I had to make a quick decision to turn sharply right at the road and probably bang into other cars, or to turn sharply left and hang tight above a steep drop-off, which would have been disastrous should we have hopped right across the road. I managed to bring the car left onto the road and follow the two ruts faithfully until I stopped the car to breathe a sigh of relief. Jonny simply said, "In Fleck we trust." All we could think of was a good hot soak in the steaming springs down at the foot of towering Mount Princeton's chalky white cliffs and a nice cup of hot tea by our campfire that night.

14

THE SOLACE OF DINOSAUR RIDGE

Quick iguanodons
Pitter pat along muddy
Beach with bright green eyes

DINOSAUR RIDGE HAS become an essential and necessary ingredient in my life since our move to Denver from a small university town on the wild and open prairies of Wyoming. Where would I have the freedom to roam and think in the urban sprawl of Denver? Where could I botanize and examine fossils? How would I stand the heat and smog of an August afternoon that would be cool and clear up in Wyoming? Where could I quickly get away from people and sirens and honking automobile horns? Piled on top of these concerns were the pressures, after a few years, of my deanship in an inner-city college with uniquely gifted yet disadvantaged students and a pressurized and strained faculty struggling with ever-shrinking budgets.

Within weeks of our arrival from Laramie, I discovered the small town of Morrison nestled behind an uplifted hogback formation called Dakota Ridge or, more fondly, Dinosaur Ridge. This magical piece of wild land lay only twenty-five minutes from central Denver. I took my first stroll along the trail, following the ridgetop well over 1,200 feet above Denver after a heavy September frost. The city lay smothered in mist and clouds and completely disappeared. I breathed the ridge's fresh and bracing air above the city's layers of cloud. That first walk along the ridge I repeated over and over again from September to April for twelve years straight. Sometimes I would go solo and sometimes with my wife and family, but most often with my little dog Mini, that golden English cocker spaniel with drooping ears and alert brown eyes.

This weekly ramble had become as much a ritual for me as my weekly walks on the Laramie plains. Summertime changed the Wyoming ritual with hikes in the alluring Snowy Range and now in the Front Range of Colorado. The high prairies of southern Wyoming have something very much in common with Dinosaur Ridge, namely, the Laramide orogeny. Sixty- to seventy-five-million-years ago, something within the Earth's core forced prehistoric swamplands (washed by the sea) upward. If four billion years could be transposed into one human life, the Laramide orogeny raised the Rockies from sea level to almost three miles above sea level during the human equivalent of two weeks.

The high, bald prairie of southern Wyoming rests at 7,200 feet, a thousand feet higher than Dinosaur Ridge. Inner forces of our planet are still pushing this land upward perhaps an eighth of an inch every century—not quite as fast as the growth rate of the Himalayas halfway around the globe. But the Laramie plains are essentially as flat as a seabed, while Dinosaur Ridge is a high, spiny ridge with downsloping Morrison Formation of gray beach rock on its east side and bright red Dakota Formation sandstone on its west side. The extreme north side is transected by Interstate 70. Why the name Dinosaur Ridge? Dinosaurs galore! Buried within the Dakota sandstones are the bones of stegosaurs, brontosaurs, and iguanodons, discovered by Arthur Lakes in 1877. Eventually, ten quarries yielded many fossils for rival museums in Philadelphia and New Haven. Today, Dinosaur Ridge is designated a national natural landmark. There are guided and self-guided tours along the base of both sides.

I love to visit one spot on the west side of Dinosaur Ridge that exposes the imprint of a brontosaurus made millions of years ago on an ancient muddy shoreline. The beast's immense weight sunk him deep into the mud. His tracks probably filled in with algal ooze, helping to preserve the footprints in hardened mud-rock. Lower down the ridge are fossilized rib and skull bones of camarasaurs, carried by streams and deposited in deeper mud that has been hardened to sandstone and exposed by erosion to present-day viewers.

On the east side of Dinosaur Ridge lies a strangely rippled rock (formerly beach) that has been hardened to gray sandstone and tilted at a ludicrous angle of forty-five degrees. Within this beach are giant three-toed tracks of a vegetarian dinosaur known as the iguanodon. Alongside his prints are three-toed prehistoric bird prints of an ostrich-like dinosaur. Early morning shadows fill the tracks, clearly revealing their deep imprint. Scientists have applied a light gray paint to the tracks so that the visitor can clearly see them no matter what time of day. Because the beach is no longer sand but rock, and because the beach lies at an extreme angle, it is difficult to imagine a sea-level beach with heavy, humid air and swampy vegetation.

On one occasion, I took a quick walk along the east side of Dinosaur Ridge at sunset before boarding a jet the next morning bound for Charleston, South Carolina, to celebrate my late brother's sixty-fifth birthday. Within hours of my arrival, I walked the Edisto Swamp Trail not far from the Georgia line with my brother and his children and their families. The geographic juxtaposition hit home. Here in Edisto Swamp I breathed heavy, vaporous air, while hours earlier I breathed the bracing air of the high desert. At Edisto, I marveled at the delicate perfection of form and color of swamp orchids, the lush array of ferns and vine-covered southern pines, and the profusion of palmettos. On Dinosaur Ridge hours earlier, wind blew through the needles of pinyons and junipers. Deep in Edisto, I smelled mud and phosphates and thick vegetation. Up on Dinosaur, I smelled dust and rock and the scent of sage. Edisto provided a secure home for dinosaur-like alligators and other reptiles like the cottonmouth water moccasin.

Alligators, incidentally, are a species 60 million years old. Their ancient ancestors lived when dinosaurs did! Edisto became for me prehistoric, Precambrian Colorado, whose oozing muds would eventually harden and be uplifted to some future multilayered Dinosaur Ridge.

Interstate 70 cuts through Dinosaur Ridge and exposes all the layers of hardened, pre-Laramide orogeny sand and mud. As dinosaur-like trucks and RVs revved their engines up I-70, Mini and I walked through a hundred million years of time. We stared up at the cut-through formations ranging in color from gray to black to red to brown and yellow. Even though the heavy traffic of I-70 roared like a troop of dinosaurs, we managed to journey backwards in time.

I let myself dream of what things looked like 300 million years ago during the early Pennsylvanian Period, with its carboniferous jungles. I imagined looking westward to see an ancient mountain range 240 million years older than the present-day Rockies. This mountain range, like any other, had streams gushing off its slopes, depositing reddish quartz sand, silt grains, and clay. I tried to imagine these reddish deposits hardening into the red sandstone of the Fountain Formation and the Red Rocks Amphitheatre of Beatles fame. But the only beetles I envisioned were black, creeping things on the muddy ooze of shorelines. What must it have been like 140 million years ago during the Jurassic Period? I imagined not seeing I-70 anymore and hearing the howl of meat-eating dinosaurs thumping through swamps and wetlands in an insufferably dank and humid atmosphere. What happened to Colorado? The only hint of its future existence lay in the gray and green and maroon claystone that would become the Morrison Formation.

I pictured in my mind escaping from wretched beasts to arrive at the late Cretaceous Period about 75 million years ago. Those frightening beasts hadn't yet left the scene, but now a great inland sea lapped the shore with tidal ripples in the mud covered by seaweed. The air remained heavy with no mountain breezes—just a flat swamp with bright, green-eyed iguanodons pitter-patting along the mud in search of lush, fern-like cycads. Gigantic feathered beasts flapped their awkward wings above my head and cackled with a combination of the sound of mythological harpies and modern-day sandhill cranes. The tan, dark gray, and black shales oozed with mud and slimy oils. I see that Mini has stepped into a mud puddle, and once again I hear the roar of I-70.

What I like most about Dinosaur Ridge is the relative peace and calm on top of its rocky spine. Up there grow yuccas, cacti, Gambel oaks, pinyon pines, Utah junipers, sagebrush, mountain mahogany, kinnikinnick, golden banner, harebells, and scores of other wildflowers. Sailing overhead are ravens, hawks, golden eagles, and swallows. Nearby are buzzing hummingbirds *(oiseaux mouches,* as they are called in French). Mini, a ground-level cocker spaniel, simply loves it up here on the ridge between September and April, when there are no rattle-snakes to worry about. She loves to peer over the edge of cliffs and stare into space as though she were going into Zen. All I have to say is "go see!" and she runs to the edge and takes it all in. She stops and listens to chickadees going "chick-a-dee-dee-dee." She eyeballs each pine squirrel scampering up a twisted tree trunk. Even when she squats to urinate, she's all eyes for what's going on around her. Yes, she's a worthy successor to the dinosaurs of old.

At a certain narrow point on the trail's crest, I often stop and feel the tex-ture of a rock, rippled and uplifted from that inland sea of a million years ago. Algal materials covered earlier ripples and preserved their form when beaches became buried under layers of other deposits that hardened to rock. Tidal rip-ples are amazing to behold millions of years later—more amazing, in a sense, than the sarcophagus of the Emperor Charlemagne, or the Rosetta Stone. Why? Sixty million years! Imagine finding a 60-million-year-old plant grow-ing in your back yard. How can one fathom the meaning of a wilderness of time found in 60 million years? A sand ripple is as common on the receded sea delta of the Colorado River down in Mexico as it was on the Great Inland Sea of ancient interior Colorado. But 60 million years separate these two sets of ripples. Ripples we can understand, but the time in between may be impossi-ble. Or is it? We do have that special gift of Kantian intuition and Thoreauvian imagination. Denver is but an intertidal city in geologic time. Dreams can cut through time like lightning through clouds to illuminate an otherwise darkened land. The numbers 60, 60 million, and 60 billion do not defy the human spirit. We can even imagine various species of dinosaurs having green flesh with bright orange spots.

I remember driving up I-70 one extremely windy day to an early January conference site on Lookout Mountain above Denver. Flames raced up the northeast slope of Dinosaur Ridge. Pinyon trees blazed with sparks that hopped up the ridge in a spectacle of beauty and terror. The blackened vegetation below the flames stood phantom-like in marked contrast to the whiteness of snow. Within days of my conference, Mini and I walked along that ridgetop to inspect the damage. Mini sniffed the air and ground all the while once we arrived at darkened soil and blackened pine branches. Even snow had become dark with black and gray ashes, making for fertile soil next spring. Not too much damage here.

One mild February weekend we had a surprise visit from our son. My wife, Maura, and I packed a lunch for the three of us, with treats for Mini, to take advantage of the warm pre-spring sunshine up on Dinosaur Ridge. Buds laced the branches of bare scrub oaks, and the most delicate and tiny flowers of sandworts sprung up close to the ground at our feet like miniature dots of snow. Arriving at a high sandstone upthrust, we stopped for lunch. The foothills of the Rockies spread westward and upward, obscuring the high Front Range. We could clearly see that our ridge protruded skyward as an un-eroded shell fragment of an outer layer of sandstone and shale that once covered the Rocky Mountains. We finished our lunch atop the layers of time by recollecting our own family layers of time when Rich was a boy in Laramie with his two sisters, Michelle and Maureen. We all had a good reunion up there on the ridge. Rich now lived in Seattle and his two sisters in New York and Fort Lauderdale—as spread apart as sediment from the Rockies that had traveled down prairie streams to the sea.

One crisp autumn day I hiked solo over the ridge when oak leaves had changed to bright scarlet. They rustled like prayer flags in the Himalayas. High in the foothills across the way, tongues of aspen blazed with a golden fire. Gray clouds swooped upslope like volcanic clouds millions of years ago when tectonic plates collided within the Laramide orogeny. During our civilized state, we humans have experienced very little volcanism. Vesuvius, Etna, Krakatoa, Mount Saint Helens, and Icelandic Eyafjallajokull were or are tiny firecrackers compared to the eruptions of the Yellowstone Caldera 600,000 years ago, when our primitive continent lay blackened for months and years on end. How frightening it must have been to see whole ranges of volcanoes puffing and exploding red-hot lava.

Snow sprinkled down from the upsloping clouds and gathered in windy wisps along my trail. A yellow-jacket wasp buzzed for cover among the last of the autumnal flowers still barely in bloom. It snowed yet harder in chilling winds, and the sky darkened. It felt good to be up here; I could have easily been hundreds of miles away. It grew even colder, and some leaves blew off the scrub oaks. My hands and feet grew numb, and it was time to make my descent to the cares of the city below. Chickadees along the trail chirped to bid me farewell.

Yes, I'm glad I discovered a place called Dinosaur Ridge. Up there, my urban-encased being is truly energized and revitalized. It is a place of magic— magical realism. It is a place that allows the spirit to roam free through time and space.

15

RAMBLES ALONG THE MOSQUITO RANGE

Views from the Mosquito Range are phenomenal. Look across the valley to the west and you see Mount Elbert and Mount Massive, usually blanketed with snow, rising above 14,400 feet as Colorado's two highest peaks. To the southwest loom Princeton, Antero, and La Plata, and northwesterly rises Mount of the Holy Cross. Directly to the east, the climber gets a bird's-eye view of Pikes Peak. Yet, when I first saw the Mosquito Range in the distance from the top of storm-wracked Mount Ida, those peaks, too, looked amazingly tall and snow-blanketed, and, no wonder; five of them rise above 14,000 feet, six if you count the spur ridge of Cameron Peak. I knew I must explore them someday, not realizing that it would be more than thirty years after my ranger days. Usually the middle three peaks of the Mosquito Range—Lincoln, Bross, and Democrat—can be climbed in one day as one has to descend at least 1,000 feet between peaks before they can count as having been climbed and that is the case between each of these three peaks. Way above Kite Lake, there is one enticing spur ridge between Democrat and Lincoln called Cameron Peak; if climbed as the only objective of the day, it counts as a fourteener. The northernmost peak is Quandary Peak, just outside of Breckenridge, and the southernmost is Mount

Sherman, which some mountaineers who, perhaps, have recently climbed Crestone Needle, consider a joke. It is nothing more than a high green hump. But so, too, is Mount Bross, only Bross is a higher green hump that bears amazing resemblance to Green Mountain, a prairie ridge that rises to the east of Dinosaur Ridge. All of these mountains were heavily mined for gold and silver, traces of which can still be found in slag heaps beneath ant-hole mines that fairly well prickle the side of Mount Democrat. But don't be fooled by "fool's gold," or iron pyrite, which will crackle and pop under a blowtorch flame. On the Leadville side of the Mosquitos, the mountains are being gouged by gigantic molybdenum mines at Climax. Molybdenum is a light metal used for constructing the bodies of jet aircraft. Mount Lincoln pitches high above the valleys below, with its dark pyramid of rocks forming the very top of the peak.

Permit me to begin with Mount Sherman. Yes, it's far less of a challenge than Crestone Needle (which requires rope and pitons), but it does provide a workout, surely more so than Mount Evans from Summit Lake. In fact, it proved to be a challenge for the women with whom I climbed one day—the first time ever that all of my companions were female, including my wife and two doctors, one from Maine (Allison) and the other from Texas (Crystal). The doctor from Augusta, Maine, developed a breathing problem at about 13,000 feet. She slowed down to a crawl, and we all stopped for her to rest. After Allison drank some hot tea, she perked up and continued her slow, methodical trek. Crystal served as her coach with words of encouragement, especially after Allison said she couldn't make it. Within thirty minutes, Maura and I stood on the final approach to the summit just a tad over 14,000 feet and waved back down to Allison and Crystal to show them they had but a little way to go. I turned back to rejoin the two doctors and walked slowly with Allison, allowing Crystal to summit with Maura. When Allison saw nothing but sky above a stony ridge, she knew she could make it, and that she did. We all applauded her as she wearily walked up to the cairn and breathed a sigh of relief at 14,036 feet. Refreshed with cheddar cheese, crackers, and tea, we all stood up to enjoy the distant view of the Sawatch Range, beginning with Tabeguache Peak and rolling northward to the Mount of the Holy Cross. Allison regained that sparkle in her eye as she stared out into endless alpine terrain and sky.

The wind picked up and a band of thick, gray clouds formed and spread from the west, making us all a bit anxious. We donned sweaters and parkas as the temperature dropped by several degrees. It was time to make our descent. We easily hopped down the stony trail to a saddle overlooking an abandoned mine. The sky grew grayer. Tufts of sunflowers bobbed in the wind. Pikas squeaked as if to warn us to quicken our pace. Just as we approached the old gold mine far above the winding gravel road back to Fairplay, it began to spit sleet and rain. We put on our baseball caps and trotted down the last bit of slick ridge to arrive at the road and our car in a torrential downpour. Mount Sherman proved to be challenge enough.

My daughter Maureen from Florida had not yet climbed a 14,000-foot peak. My son, Rich, had not yet ascended Mount Democrat. The three of us and my son's dog, Boo Radley, departed for Alma early in August while my wife babysat our three grandchildren. We turned onto the Kite Lake road and quickly gained elevation up to 12,900 feet, switching back and forth past abandoned gold mines and splashing through streams. All the while, Boo sniffed the air and constantly yawned noisily in anticipation of our arrival. Anticipatory yawns, I call them. Not a cloud in the sky! Kite Lake glistened in the rising sun. The air was chilly.

My Floridian daughter (some ten years after the Sand Hills hike), bundled up in a heavy sweater and hooded parka, while Rich and I shouldered our packs and began our climb. We stopped along the trail to admire bright-yellow sunflowers and light-blue harebells, but not Boo. He dashed up and down the slope at least six times. Ravens circled above, letting out raucous squawks that echoed for miles. Pikas and marmots squeaked and whistled as we climbed up to another abandoned mining shack surrounded with small stalks of alpine bistort. Up here, the temperature was even chillier. We put on our gloves and proceeded up toward the saddle between Cameron and Democrat. Halfway there, we stopped for a bit of trail mix and admired the view of kite-shaped

Kite Lake far below. We couldn't help but notice numerous mining scars above, some silver in appearance, some golden. Boo dashed ahead to wait for us, along with dozens of other dogs, at the saddle. We three slogged along, stopping now and then to catch our breath. But not Boo! He stood patiently, cocking his head, up at the saddle. When we finally arrived, Rich rewarded Boo with a treat, and we rewarded ourselves with small chocolate bars as we stood and gazed at the mountainous terrain to the west, at huge Mount Democrat rising to the south, and at Cameron Peak looming to the north. A far cry from sawgrass and palmettos of Maureen's Florida!

Somehow I had remembered gentle switchbacks going up Mount Democrat a few years earlier with our neighbors Mike and Crystal. But that was an illusion. Instead, the trail proved to be quite steep, with loose gravel, rolling stones, and tricky switchbacks. Boo had no problems. We three trudged along, carrying on a conversation that was constantly interrupted by huffs and puffs. This side of the mountain remained devoid of almost any vegetation. The wind increased as the temperature decreased. At last we saw people resting against the sky a few hundred feet higher. They stood, of course, on a false summit, and Boo soon joined them.

"What kind of dog is he?" they asked.

"Part border collie and part Lab. See his webbed feet?" Rich answered.

Meanwhile, the beast dashed off to the left of the trail to sniff rocks where other dogs had paid liquid homage. Once Maureen arrived at this ridgeline, we pointed up at the last bit of summit atop a hundred-foot pile of rocky slabs. Dutifully, we hoofed onward, trying to keep up with Boo, until we stood at the very summit. There we high-fived with Maureen to celebrate her first fourteener at 14,148 feet, or slightly more than two and a half miles above her home in Pembroke Pines, Florida. It was a great occasion for our family as we gazed around at a full sweep of mountainous space.

On another occasion, Cameron Peak, across the way from Democrat, was our goal as Maura and I hopped out of the car at Kite Lake with our neighbors Mike and Crystal. We had planned this climb as a farewell get-together with them since they were moving to Oregon a few days later. We had to make the climb on July 1, a tad early for completely summer conditions. From Kite Lake we looked up at deep, menacing banks of snow lining the trail, even covering it. Nonetheless, we proceeded up to the abandoned mine without any difficulty. Alpine avens and snow buttercups sprouted out of the edge of the melting snow. The sky was azure blue and the temperature a bit chilly. We all put on our gloves and continued huffing until our trail led us right into a very large and deep snowfield. Above, it looked clear pretty much up to the saddle. Mike and I broke a narrow pathway for the women by wading up to our knees and sometimes up to our hips. Maura seemed frightened. To alleviate her fears, I walked above Maura while Mike walked below her, each of us holding one of her arms. We hobbled slowly for fifty yards and caught her if she slipped until we got to open land once again. We returned to Crystal, who was twenty-five years younger than Maura, and got her through the large bank of snow quite quickly. Maura, in the meantime, had become hesitant about continuing upslope, but we assured her that she had gotten through the worst of it. Fortunately, the trail remained open all the way to the saddle, where we rested and ate snacks. The view back to sparkling Kite Lake proved rewarding. A few more climbers trudged through the broken snow below, waving thanks to us for clearing the way.

We easily avoided smaller patches of snow on the way up to Cameron's summit, but our legs were a bit tired after the snowy episode below. We hardly noticed frail chiming bells blowing in a gentle breeze along the switchbacks. Red-tailed hawks swooped over the higher ridgelines. We talked of our friends' move to Oregon and our trip the following year to Ireland, Maura's homeland. Mike asked if there were any hills to climb back there. "Not like this," I said. But I explained there's nothing prettier than the green and lush Mountains of Mourne in County Down. They are carpeted with pink fields of heather and occasional patches of lush, sweet blaeberries that taste like our blueberries. On the flanks of Slieve Gullion, one of the Mountains of Mourne, there is a dense plantation of new forests resembling what ancient Ireland must have looked like when Celtic tribesmen hunted stag deer and black bears. Except now, as I explained to our neighbors, the forests consist of Alaskan Sitka spruce and Norway pines. Yes, those rolling green Mountains of Mourne sweep right down to the sea, said Maura paraphrasing the lyrics of a song.

A sudden gust of icy wind brought us all right back to Colorado. Trail dust blew in swirls into our eyes and nostrils. We at last reached the upper spiny ridge, and it was an easy hop up to the snowless summit at 14,238 feet. We found a hollow that was out of the wind and stretched out on the ground to rest our weary bones. Then we sat up and ate some cheese and salami sandwiches and drank hot tea. Restored, Mike and I got up to look across at the high pyramid of Mount Lincoln rising to the north, but as time was fleeting, and they had to finish packing for Oregon, we slowly made our descent to the saddle and through the snowfield back to Kite Lake when nothing was left but memories.

And what of Lincoln and Bross? I had earlier climbed both of them solo via the same route up the saddle and to the crest of Cameron, but on this occasion I pushed on to Mount Lincoln by way of a charming piece of tundra tucked below the north face of Cameron, with Mount Lincoln rising a mile away. I had discovered a marvelous bit of alpine tundra desert with a whole colony of miniature alpine mullein sprinkled with a few pink blossoms bursting forth from fleshy rosettes of greenish, felt-like leaves growing out of the stony soil. I had never before seen such a profusion of vegetation growing at an altitude of or above 14,000 feet. I felt like staying here the rest of the day just to enjoy this bit of a microclimate so high in the sky.

But I forged ahead following the trail that connected Cameron to Lincoln at the very edge of the western ridgeline where the land abruptly dropped off several thousand feet down into glacial cirques packed with snow and ice fields. Within half an hour, I found myself climbing the last bit of a rocky summit, which involved a few foot- and handholds, until I stood atop Mount Lincoln at 14,286 feet, 30 feet higher than Longs Peak and the eighth highest peak in Colorado. I peered straight down into an endless abyss separating Lincoln from Quandary Peak, with its long incline and final hump of a summit.

I remember having climbed Quandary on the latest date ever for a four-teener—mid-September—with the late Mark Reames. On the way up, under the clearest of skies, we admired browning tundra peppered with alpine gentians and dwarf rosy paintbrushes. It was a splendid day. Mark Reames and I talked of our experiences in Japan and that, although we didn't know each other at that time, we lived across the Nigawa River from one another. Sometimes the Reames family noticed an American family carrying groceries on the other side of the river and wondered who they might be. We met eight years later as colleagues at Teikyo Loretto Heights University, a Colorado branch of a Japanese university. Mark and I worked on developing a "Colorado Experience" curriculum for first-year Japanese students. Colorado would be the focus not only in writing classes but also in history, photography, and biology classes. All faculty would get together with students on Saturday field trips up Mount Evans, where students would keep journals describing the krummholz zone of bristlecone pines. They would collect and press plant specimens, take black-and-white landscape photographs, and read Enos Mills and other Front Range writers to gain historical perspectives on earlier-day Colorado. They had to write narrative papers on what it is like being on the side and top of Mount Evans. One student wrote a paper for my English class saying, "Trees on Mount Evans are shaped by the wind. *No.* They *are* the wind!"

"Did you ever do anything like that with Japanese students in Japan?" asked Mark.

"No, but I did things like that with my family, for sure."

"Did you ever climb any mountains in Japan besides Fuji San?" he asked.

"Yes, quite a few coastal hills, including Miyajima Yama, Kabutoyama—an extinct volcano near our home—and Rokko Mountain. I remember climbing up Rokko San on the trail of the fire Buddhas. I couldn't get over how thick the cobwebs were between forest trees. They actually crackled as you passed through them."

Mark laughed.

"I remember walking very gingerly when I spotted a deadly poisonous *mamushi,* a viper snake that is brownish-black in color. He wound his way uphill parallel to me until I arrived at the first fire Buddha overlook. Then it slid into some undergrowth beneath blazing-scarlet maple trees *(momiji-ja).* Just seeing a statue of the Buddha with flames coming out of the top of his head purified me of my fear."

"Well, there are no *mamushi* up here," Mark said gleefully as he pointed across at Mount Lincoln.

We continued our climb up to the base of the final much steeper summit when I suddenly experienced a leg cramp. Mark had a worried look on his face, hoping I would not give up on the final assault. I stomped my foot on the ground several times and the cramp thankfully disappeared. White upcroppings of shiny granite shone brightly in the September sun. They looked like marble glistening in the Italian Dolomites. We at last stood atop Quandary Peak at 14,265 feet and opened our lunch sacks. Mark surprised me with a fresh tomato (as he had done on Mount Elbert) picked from his garden that morning. We counted thirty other 14,000-foot peaks from up here, including all those in the Mosquito, Front, and Sawatch ranges.

But here I stood in the brisk air atop Mount Lincoln, gazing across at Mount Bross. What the heck, I thought. I'll go for Bross as well. The wind increased to such a velocity that I had to hold on to my sunglasses or have them ripped off my face. Once I descended to the ridge line that joined Cameron and Lincoln, the wind, mercifully, decreased from furious to steady. I followed a trail eastward toward Bross but lost even more elevation into a grassy meadow at the base of Mount Bross, which rose to 14,172 feet—104 feet lower than knobby Mount Lincoln. The meadow lay a thousand feet or so shy of the highest knoll of Mount Bross. Replenishing myself with trail mix and Gatorade, I easily bounded up the gentle incline, stopping several times to look across at Lincoln and Cameron. Sunflowers cropped up all around me, as did white clumps of alpine bistort and purple king's and rosy queen's crown, lending dots of color that resembled a Georges Seurat painting of a Parisian park. Hawks and ravens circled about, letting out high-pitched whistles or raucous squawks, respectively. A few mud tunnels lay exposed from melted snow—the workings of pocket gophers that create a miniature version of a New York subway system in winter.

I scanned the afternoon sky to see thunderheads building up over the Sawatch Mountains to the west. Time to finish my ascent and plan a route back to Kite Lake! Should I go all the way back to Cameron Peak and descend a rocky trail to the saddle between Cameron and Democrat? Or should I explore the possibility of a quicker and more direct descent straight down from Mount Bross? Several teenage boys stood at the rock cairn marking the summit, and as I approached, I waved to them. At the windy summit, I shared some trail mix with them and asked their advice on a descent route to Kite Lake. They gleefully advised me not to go all the way back to Cameron, but to simply follow the trail southeastward along the flanks of Mount Bross and then make a rapid switch-backing descent to the valley below. They mentioned that the trail would be steep and that I would sometimes have to sit and slide down, controlling my speed with my feet. Bad advice for a man in his midfifties (at that time), as I had to contend with weaker knees than teenagers had. Worse yet, with the approaching storms, I followed their advice.

The trail along the flank proved easy enough, as it descended at a very gradual rate. Once I arrived at the south side of Bross with a bird's-eye view down to sparkling Kite Lake, I had to make a sharp descent to a lower spiny ridge that jutted out over the valley. In order to do this, I sat down and slid on the seat of my pants for thirty minutes until I reached the plateau below. But the kids didn't say which way to go from here—right or left? The trail forked and went both ways. I chose the right side facing Cameron Peak. I descended on wobbly knees until the pitch became nearly vertical! I sat down again and inched my way very cautiously, thinking to myself that this could not be the trail. If only I had my usual trail companions with me! I happened to spot the tiniest of human figures far below. This ant-sized figure seemed to be signaling. But signaling what? I took off my sunglasses and squinted at this figure. What the heck was he or she trying to say? Then it dawned on me that the person was violently waving his or her arms upward toward me. I got it! Slowly I inched my way backward, daring not to turn around. When I say inched, I mean inched. It took me more than an hour to slowly scuttle back up to the plateau overlooking Kite Lake. Perhaps guardian angels can appear in the tiniest of forms. Once up there, I tearfully noticed that clearly the trail to the left was more heavily used. Someone needs to put a branch across the trail to the right! (Later, I did just this.) Although I had to sit down and slide on the seat of my pants, I did so with a big grin on my face, because now I could see a series of switchbacks a hundred feet below me. Arriving at the first switchback, I gave thanks and enjoyed every foot of the way down. I stopped frequently to admire crinkly monument plants, spongy moss, springy elk sedge, and an ever enlarging Kite Lake. It was amazing to see dwarf spruce and willows at my feet; amazing to breathe rain-soaked air to the west; amazing to hear rumbles of thunder miles away; and amazing to hear distant human voices from the trail far below me. Western song sparrows chirped. Very fat marmots waddled across the rocky terrain before me.

It was simply great to arrive at more level tundra that was soft underfoot. I smiled at everyone I passed along the shoreline of Kite Lake—no longer a gleaming little eye in the tundra seen from thousands of feet above. Solo climbs are indeed spirit builders, but they can be more risky than they are worth. I had no trouble that night falling into a deep sleep!

16

MULTIPLE ASCENTS OF MOUNT EVANS AND PIKES PEAK

YEARS AGO MY PARENTS and I wound our way up a twisting mountain road in my 1939 Chevrolet. I had taken the day off as a park ranger naturalist in Rocky Mountain National Park to show my visiting parents some rugged alpine terrain outside the national park and much higher than Trail Ridge Road—in fact, the highest paved auto road in North America. This road led us up Mount Evans to 14,200 feet, 64 feet below the summit. To get to the actual summit, we had to climb a winding dirt trail for 64 vertical feet to the USGS bench mark at the top. Only a day ago we all had felt the distant tremors of the great 1959 earthquake in Yellowstone. We certainly hoped we would not experience an aftershock up here on this narrow, winding road, with no bumper rails separating our moving tires from a 2,000-foot drop-off just like the Mount Princeton road. My mother's eyes showed fear, if not panic, as I steered the car around each sharp turn on the way to Summit Lake just shy of 13,000 feet. I tried to calm her by pointing out the window at fields of alpine sunflowers that were almost as yellow as the sun itself.

"Keep both hands on the wheel," she said, while she secretly prayed for a level stretch of road.

My father, on the other hand, was all eyes for the vast panorama of prairie that spread far below, forming a great arc of horizon. He mumbled to himself, "God, what country!"—an important statement since he considered himself agnostic.

"What are those animals?" he asked suddenly as we wound around a curve.

"Rocky Mountain goats," I said with a gleam in my eye.

My mother immediately seemed to calm down when she rolled the window down to stare into their brown eyes after I stopped the car. She was simply amazed at their gracefulness and beauty as they danced through a snowfield as white as their coats. She started to laugh when she recalled repeating what one smart-aleck graduate student told her back in Princeton—that nature had marvelously accommodated mountain goats' anatomy to mountains by giving them two shorter legs on one side so they could more easily walk around steep slopes. She had naively repeated this bit of information once in Parnassus Bookshop when there was a lull in the conversation among poets and professors. The poet John Berryman had roared with laughter, saying, "What happens if they change their direction?" We drove a bit farther with smiles on our faces to the Summit Lake parking area and got out of the car to take a wee ramble.

Out on the solid, flower-strewn tundra, which was so antithetical to smoggy, industrialized New Jersey, my parents began to relax and take it all in. We had brought along some sandwiches and a thermos of coffee, and when we arrived at some flat gray rocks, I suggested we sit down for a tundra picnic overlooking miles of muskegs—a marshy series of ponds and connecting streams—that are very much part of Jack London's stories of the Far North. This was their first trip west of Harrisburg, Pennsylvania. They, of course, underwent a kind of "shock of geography," but the longer they remained above 12,800 feet, the more accustomed they became to this new land—especially with the rather awesome glacial cirque of Mount Evans forming a backdrop. There was nothing back east to begin to compare with the vastness of the Rocky Mountain West. They never had the opportunity of seeing Mount Katahdin rising high above tree line in northern Maine, although my father had done some rambles along the misty Appalachian Trail in the White Mountains of New Hampshire. Rugged though the White Mountains are, they just don't quite measure up to the vastness of the titanic Rockies that stretch from the Canadian to the Mexican borders.

After lunch, and after delighting in a close inspection of miniature alpine forget-me-nots, I suggested we drive up to the summit of Mount Evans. Although a bit of fear returned to my mother's eyes, she and Dad seemed resolved to continue up the highest paved road in North America since they had mastered their fears of 12,200-foot Trail Ridge Road just the other day in Rocky Mountain National Park. I had selected this piece of terrain so that they could experience—for the first time ever—life above 14,000 feet.

Once they stood at the benchmark of 14,264 feet and stared out into planetary space, I knew they were hooked on the American West, where they would retire a few years later. They would open up a mail-order antiquarian bookshop in Laramie in the spirit of old Parnassus Bookshop in Princeton twenty years earlier, and would even have numerous walk-in customers. You can bet that they stocked western Americana, even my first book of poems, *Palms, Peaks, and Prairies* (1967).

~

Some thirty years after this car trip, I had the occasion to lead groups of Japanese students from Teikyo Loretto Heights University in Denver along the tundra beneath the summit of Mount Evans. We traveled up there in rickety old school buses whose engines overheated with steam pouring out. While they cooled down, my group of students, doing their "Colorado Experience," squatted down to make pen-and-ink sketches of delicate alpine vegetation. Such sketches would line the borders of their English compositions written about the alpine heights of Colorado. Like my parents, they, too, had to overcome the "shock of geography" since most of them came from the inner city of Tokyo. Other groups took photographs or botanized, depending on which instructor they were with. As it became late afternoon, the air temperature dropped considerably. I suggested that my students (who were learning "beyond the blackboard") and teaching assistant finish taking notes for their future compositions and finish their sketching quickly. In fact, we were the last group on the mountain as we strolled back to our school bus. The driver nervously informed us rather solemnly that our bus was broken down. He had worked on it all afternoon, to no avail. He was going to wait for the tow truck. Now it was quite chilly, with the sun being a mere red ball on the western horizon. What were we to do? Fortunately, my teaching assistant, Tony Tadasa, spoke fluent Japanese. He explained to the coeds that they must forget their false pride and hitchhike back to Echo Lake Lodge, far below. He finally succeeded in getting some of them to stick out their thumb and hitch a ride, but there were very few tourists left up there in darkening skies. In fact, nine of us remained tundra-bound. What would we do? If only we could shape-shift into mountain goats. They really needed warmer jackets to begin hoofing downslope from around 13,800 feet to Echo Lake Lodge over 2,000 feet lower. Nonetheless, we began our cold hike down.

Something told my Teikyo colleague, Reuben Ellis, that all was not well up on the mountain. Even though he was speeding past Idaho Springs on the interstate, he decided to turn around and drive back up in his four-wheel-drive Wagoneer. We had all managed to descend by a half mile or so when Reuben suddenly appeared. I have never seen such wide smiles on students' faces. All nine of us crowded in—some sitting in the cargo section, others jammed into tiny spaces—and we happily journeyed back to the city of Denver, all reiterating our experience in both languages.

After my Teikyo years came a series of climbs with different people starting at Summit Lake at 12,800 feet. Once it was with my wife, along with Michael and Ellen Mackey; another time was with my son and his dog, Boo; another was with Scott Martens, my Iowa niece's husband; and yet another was with Gordon and Jean Fader, my niece Missy, and Missy's husband, John. On that occasion I served as guide for an otherwise entirely sea level crew. Gordon, of course, had climbed with me in snow and sleet on our failed attempt of Mount Princeton and successful climbs in Maine and Arizona, but all the others had never climbed a mountain of any sort before. And yet, they all did incredibly well, especially in crossing a snowfield at a thirty-degree angle. Jean, the artist, brought along her sketch pad for the summit and had a photograph taken of her sketching at 14, 264 feet—all smiles. But the going down proved quite tiring to all of them. Their knees became wobbly, and their stomachs growled like coyotes. Although Jean limped a bit on the way down to the parking area at Summit Lake, she would never have given up such an experience on this cloudless day in July. Gordon was pleased as punch to have made four climbs with me—Katahdin, Wilson, part-way up Princeton, and Evans. My niece and her husband returned to Charleston, South Carolina, with a fourteener under their belts.

The most memorable climb of Evans was with my wife, Maura, and our dog, Mini. We didn't simply climb directly up from Summit Lake, but went all the way around the glacial cirque and approached the summit from the west side for an all-day hike. Backpacks shouldered, we hoofed around to the western shoreline of the lake and its marsh marigolds and proceeded up a series of rocky humps well above 13,000 feet. Each ledge we crossed lay embossed with beds of alpine flowers, including bright-blue dwarf columbines growing out of rocky crevices.

We paused to drink water, eat trail mix, and throw Mini her treat. Just over the next ledge we gained a broad view of a very green plateau. Four mountain goats grazed in the distance, and Mini cautiously kept her distance. This piece of terrain reminded me so much of Medicine Bow Peak west of Laramie. My mind drifted back to the early 1970s, when my son was just five years old.

~

West of Laramie and east of Saratoga, an alpine haven humps upward over 12,000 feet, laced with named and unnamed lakes that are surrounded by creaking spruce and Indian paintbrush, and where hawks are always circling high above. No matter what the season, those glittering snowfields look like some vast Moby Dick rising up from the rolling prairie floor. Their lure is hard to resist. Up there in the Snowies, the alpine seasons fuse with summer that bursts into fall, which is snatched by winter gripping the approaching spring.

One morning late in July, as I played ball in the backyard with my little boy Rich, we couldn't help but glance westward toward Medicine Bow Peak.

"How would you like to climb Medicine Bow today, Rich?

"Is it hard to climb?"

"It's a joy to climb."

We packed our lunch and soon found ourselves on the winding trail above Lewis Lake. Putting on our sweaters in the biting chill of the wind, we passed patches of pink "watermelon" snow gleaming under an intense sun. I remember years back tasting some of that red-algae-ridden snow and soon suffering nausea and aching bones for three long days. Rich didn't dare even whiff a handful of pink snow, although I told him it smelled just like a watermelon cut open.

When we reached the saddle beneath Medicine Bow Peak and the Sugar Loaf, my son asked, "Do you think I can make it" He looked a bit tired, but I encouraged him to climb up the switchbacked trail through evergreen brush and scrawny stands of willow to a spot overlooking Lewis Lake. Here we had our sandwiches and hard-boiled eggs coated with salt and pepper. We ate fresh oranges for dessert, and did that trickling juice ever taste good to our parched mouths! Afternoon thunderheads slowly built up as we got up and started our gradual trek upward. Little swallows flicked past our heads. Rich wanted to take frequent rests, but after an hour of steady progress, we came to the edge of a steep snowfield, where we had to inch our way straight up, cutting steps as we went. At one very steep pitch, I carried my boy a few hundred feet. His weariness completely disappeared from his face as he crawled across the last hump of snow to the summit. It was good to see the joy in his eyes as he looked north at Elk Mountain, with a rumbling thunderhead hovering just above it.

~

Mini barked several times at a fluttering raven over her head. I asked Maura if she didn't think this spot on Mount Evans looked like the Snowy Range up in Wyoming. She agreed, and we reminisced about our annual Labor Day climb of Medicine Bow Peak with Rich, Michelle, and Maureen. We performed this ritual at least ten times.

"The next time Michelle and her husband, Rob, come out for a visit, we'll have to take them up Mount Evans," I said.

"Do you think we can make it all the way up this side of Evans? We've been at it for quite a while," Maura said.

"Let's give it a try."

We took another breather while looking across at a lightning-bolt-shaped snowfield that dropped off the west face of Mount Evans. The three of us proceeded over some jagged ledges and were afforded a grand view of Mount Bierstadt, rising a thousand feet higher with a steep abyss in between. Other climbers coming down from Evans told us we had less than a half mile to go. We followed the rock cairns up a forty-five degree pitch above Abyss Lake. I could tell that Maura was beginning to feel uncomfortable, especially after we had to push Mini's pumping hind legs in midair under a ledge that she couldn't quite manage on her own. We sat down for some Irish tea poured from our thermos and waved at other climbers, who told us the West Arm summit was just above us. Feeling better, Maura got up. We followed more sets of cairns and arrived at the West Arm in a matter of minutes. Mini stood at the very precipice and stared straight down at Summit Lake. Instead of hiking along the crest line over to Mount Evans' slightly higher summit, we bounced down the tundra on the back side of the mountain, crossed the highway as it wound around to the front side, and soon strolled across a gentle ridge overlooking Summit Lake. If you climb just to the West Arm, it counts as a separate fourteener, like climbing just to Cameron Peak. We all slept well that night, although once or twice poor Mini woke up whimpering.

Rich, his then-fiancée, Jess, and I chose to spend our Fourth of July climbing Pikes Peak from the west side, beginning at Crags Campground off the road to Cripple Creek. At first we had difficulty finding the trail; in fact, we never found it. We simply ascended in a southeasterly direction through a dense evergreen forest until, at long last, we emerged onto the tundra from a rather steep, rocky ridge. We heard a strange buzzing sound in the distance which proved to be racing cars! We totally spaced out the annual Fourth of July race up Pikes

Peak. We dashed across the gravel road only to see Bobby Unser's car whiz past us at some incredible speed. Despite the noise, we took time to enjoy a ground-cover of spring beauties, Parry's primroses, alpine forget-me-nots, and alpine sunflowers against a bright azure sky.

Obviously, we could not follow the gravel road up to the very summit. Instead, we traversed the plateau so far above Colorado Springs and scrambled up the last several hundred feet of ledges and boulders coated with crusty lichens. At times, our view down sheer faces of cliff proved frightening, especially with irregular gusts of wind. While we were dressed in hooded parkas up there above 13,800 feet, we couldn't help but notice the steam heat of the flat plains 9,000 feet below. No wonder this mountain generates its own weather. It is the only fourteener that rises directly up from the prairies with no foothills. As a result, cold, downsloping air collides with hot, sultry prairie air of July. Once this happens, storm clouds develop seemingly out of nowhere. I have never witnessed such violent hailstorms as I have on the Palmer Divide far below Pikes Peak. The entire ground can be covered with a thick layer of summer hail in minutes.

We stopped for a rest just one hundred feet below the summit. As expected, thunderheads built up in the distant western horizon. Jess looked a bit nervous, but I explained that going down the mountain would be considerably quicker. When we reached the summit, thankfully the car race had finished. We walked over to the restaurant and snack bar—the only fourteener in Colorado with such a facility—and I ordered three plates of jalapeño-smothered nachos and soft drinks. Rich and Jess looked at me rather doubtfully. Was I in my right mind? But we sat down, and in minutes our plates were empty.

"A strange but great choice, Dad," Rich said.

Our conversation at a 14,110-foot dining table proved to be a bit wacky. We all giggled at almost anything and seemed to have difficulty choosing words. But then thunder rumbled in the distance. We left the building quickly and started our long descent back to our car. It proved to be fairly easy descending to the plateau and following the tundra ridgeline to the point where we could see, far below, the crags of our trailhead. But which ravine should we descend? Rich discovered a trail, to our great joy, but the trail soon petered out at tree line. Rather than climbing back up, we cast our lot with the valley below and bushwhacked our way down. This proved to be quite tiring, and Jess looked worried.

To pass the time during our steady descent, I remarked that at least this going down wasn't as dangerous as the occasion I had on Slieve Gullion in Northern Ireland. They both asked me why. I explained that once while I stood atop Slieve Gullion and looked all around at the green universe of Ireland, the IRA raided a British garrison at Fork Hill in a valley directly below where my car was parked. Instead of following the winding trail back down through heather and pine, I took a shortcut, all the while listening to tracer bullets and high velocity rifle fire. Two British choppers flew directly below me and headed for the Fork Hill garrison. By the time they fired a few rounds, the raid was over and silence returned. Nonetheless, I kept descending at a rapid rate to get back to my car just above the garrison.

I dropped into a small vale to arrive in a thick, oozing peat bog with clumps of ferns and rich green moss. Part of the bog had been cut to drain. Eventually, bog farmers (the kind Thoreau mentions in *Walden*) would haul out tons of thick brown peat for turf fires in the cottages below. Black choughs flew overhead, with their orange bills highlighted in the afternoon sun. I had to be very careful taking this shortcut crossing the bog by stepping on vegetated clumps; otherwise I would sink hip-deep in watery moss. When I got across the bog, I climbed over some steep, treacherous rocks covered with thick moss. Suddenly slipping, I grabbed an exposed root as I would have done in the Rockies, but the root pulled right out of the moss, and I fell backward into a boggy hole. I went through all of this to fulfill a promise of writing an article for a small press nature journal. Worse yet, I wore a black leather jacket which, unknown to me, was the color of the IRA.

Mountaineering in Ireland requires you to take unusual precautions. Although the rifle fire had stopped completely, I wanted to get back to the car and get out of there just in case it flared up again. I finally climbed out of the bog, crossed a field laced with luscious blaeberries, and descended a steep hill to my car.

Jess asked me what I did then. In reply, I told her that I avoided the town of Fork Hill completely by following an unapproved gravel road and "jumped" the border back into the Republic of Ireland. It wasn't long until I pulled into the driveway of Maura's old home at Tullyraghan, where I told my story of the day and was at once served a tall glass of black Guinness with a creamy head and some tasty wheaten bread cut from a fresh-baked loaf.

Here on the west flank of Pikes Peak it was beginning to get dark, but we could see the rocky crags no more than a mile away. We were all quite weary as we brushed through pine branches and bramble. We could have surely enjoyed a pint of Guinness at that point. When we hopped into the car, the last traces of daylight lingered in the northwestern skies. We relived that climb all the way back to Dublin, I mean Denver.

17

PAHA SAPA WAKAN (SACRED BLACK HILLS)

I—Laramie Peak

We passed Fort Laramie in the night, and on the seventh morning out we found ourselves in the Black Hills, with Laramie Peak at our elbow . . . looming vast and solitary—a deep, dark, rich indigo blue in hue, so portentously did the old colossus frown from under his beetling brows of storm clouds.

—Mark Twain, *Roughing It*

IN MARK TWAIN'S day and earlier, Wyoming's Laramie Range was considered part of the Black Hills. About the time Mark Twain went west to the Nevada Territory on his overland stagecoach journey, a Black Hills treaty known as the Treaty of Fort Laramie was signed in 1868 by Lakota tribal leaders and federal agents, stating specifically that the Black Hills were to remain Indian territory and that whites could mine gold and carry it out via prescribed wagon roads. But under no circumstances would non-Indian settlement be allowed. For the Lakota people, the Black Hills (Paha Sapa Wakan) were and *are* the center of the universe, where the good red road and the black road of despair cross. They are a place of visions. Nicholas Black Elk, holy man of the Oglala clan of the Lakota tribe, believed that these hills held special significance. Not only were they essential to the practice of the sacred rites of his tribe, they also gathered in thunderclouds, or thunder beings, which provided him and others with a special vision to help his people remain whole.

In order to acquaint myself with these sacred mountains, how could I ignore Wyoming's old Black Hills? No better place to start than Laramie Peak, considered by some to have the most classic pyramidal shape of any mountain in the West. Pink puffs of clouds fleeced the eastern horizon of Laramie, Wyoming, as I drew the curtains aside and awaited my climbing partner, Dick Barbour. After a second cup of coffee, I hopped in his jeep, and Dick and I forged northward toward 10,274-foot Laramie Peak in the balmy air of dawn. A haze hugged the Snowy Range to the west, putting to mind Henry Thoreau's poem "Woof of the Sun, Ethereal Gauze," which is woven of "Nature's richest stuffs." The pink clouds gradually whitened with the rising sun, and mountain bluebirds fluttered along the telephone wires.

Distant, dark Laramie Peak remained remote until we turned onto a prairie gravel road north of Rock River and drove directly toward the mountain. The entire Laramie Range spread southward from Laramie Peak, looking quite bald with only a few vegetated spots here and there. I remember camping up there once, south of Laramie Peak, with my family in a sheltered aspen grove, to be awakened several times by hooting owls under starry skies until dawn came with the distant Snowy Range turning pinkish-red. On other occasions we would go up into these hills to gather ripe chokecherries to make a nice tart and wild pancake syrup inspired by our Shoshone friends.

Now, a covey of sage hens strutted in front of our jeep as we proceeded up a prairie knoll. They seemed so unaware of our presence, vehicle and all, that we could have thrown pebbles at them and they would not have flinched. Several pronghorn antelope bobbed up and down as they danced across the prairie, catching sunlight on their white rumps. As we turned onto the Garret

Road considerably northeast of Rock River, Wyoming, we immediately became aware of a change in landscape. Rolling prairie gave way to upcroppings of granite dotted with jack pines, somewhat reminiscent of South Dakota. More and more knife-shaped rock hills appeared here and there as we bounced along the dusty road.

To me, the country before us appeared as what I imagined the Australian Outback to look like, but instead of wallabies and kangaroos, antelope grazed along dried-up streambeds. Dick and I became so entranced by this "down under" landscape that we missed our turn and had to backtrack to pick up the Laramie Peak road. We drove up a steep hill overlooking a ranch house just like the one in the movie *The Big Country,* only without Charles Bickford sitting on the porch with a Winchester rifle. Forest lands lay a few miles directly to our east. After opening and closing several barbed-wire fence gates, we drove on toward Bear Creek and in a matter of minutes, suddenly plunged down into the creek, worrying if we would ever get across. But the jeep bounced up over a steep eastern bank and bounded into a dense, trembling aspen grove, with Laramie and Eagle Peaks looming high above. The aspen leaves fluttered like some sort of spirit beings.

Large, sweet, vanilla-smelling ponderosa pines rose into the sky all around us. We crossed several soft meadows of tall grass, sunflowers, and fireweed. A mile later, we arrived at Friend Park, a grassy meadow surrounded with lodgepole pines, ponderosa pines, and aspen trees. The air was sweet and warm as we put on our hiking gear to proceed up the five-mile trail to the summit of Laramie Peak.

Pine squirrels scurried along the branches above our heads as we scuttled up the trail. A young mule deer pranced through the ferny woods in a vale just below us. We began to feel like we belonged to the land especially after feasting on juicy wild raspberries and tiny pink grouseberries that peppered the vines at trailside. High, slightly reddish cliffs loomed above—we could even hear the wind rustling through pines that clung to those cliffs several hundred feet above. With a few swigs of icy canteen water, we pushed on up the winding trail.

Canada jays and Clark's nutcrackers squawked in the dense forests as those once-high cliffs gradually sank below us.

The closer we came to the summit, the steeper the trail became, sometimes at a forty-degree angle. There were switchbacks every fifty feet. A few cascading streams tumbled out of boulder-strewn cliffs, softened with clusters of bright-blue chiming bells and Colorado columbines. Those boulders got larger and larger as we gained elevation. Where is the summit? It had to be the next pinnacle—but no. After a half hour of huffing and puffing, that next pinnacle stood far below us. Many moons later, I would make use of this experience in my novel *Clearing of the Mist,* in which Fort Laramie cavalry units pursued Indians up Laramie Peak. One of the soldiers was an Irish immigrant who saw the parallel between starving Irish during the potato famine and the tribal people having all their buffalo killed, causing him to switch sides.

Dick and I finally caught a glimpse of a relay antenna high atop the bald peak still above us. We stopped to rest and drink more water. The trail became steeper and more winding. But with a final spurt of energy, we clambered over the last hump and out onto the narrow ridge that overlooked a quarter of the state of Wyoming.

Hazy valleys below gleamed in the sun. Distant Elk Mountain to the west darkened in a patch of cloud. The Snowy Range to the southwest and Casper Mountain to the northwest spread before us. We couldn't help but notice dark, pine-strewn ridges fingering their way eastward all the way to the rising Black Hills of South Dakota. Surely these old territorial Black Hills were truly connected to those of South Dakota. The exhilarating air we breathed helped us forget the tiresome agony of the trail below. We nibbled on fresh peaches and sandwiches, which restored our energy as we chatted with a few other fellow climbers who had just reached the summit—one fellow for his fifth pilgrimage. He pointed out a hermit's shack in a hazy valley far below—an ideal place for solitude and contemplation in noisy modern times.

Distant thunder rumbled and growled as we signed the summit register. We hopped down the trail, doing our own mountain-spirits dance. Halfway down, thunder boomed and rumbled from cliff to cliff, and the peak itself appeared as Mark Twain described it, with a beetling brow. Sheets of hail pelted us as we trotted through fields of Indian paintbrush. Without gloves, my hands became cold and numb. All too soon we arrived at the jeep and headed back toward Laramie, nestled beneath giant thunderheads all cast aglow by the setting sun.

II—Hin Han Kaga Paha (Harney Peak)

From West to East a summer offering is made
where thunder beings, thunder beings, thunder beings,
rising white above the black of lower clouds,
catch a rosy glint from the golden West.
Up they rise, even higher, up to the Spirit,
the Great Spirit, the unifier, the unifier
sending fire down in bolts, jagged bolts,
scorching the wet green land pelted white where
grasses sway and bend in rushes of wind
and cottonwoods clitter in torrents of rain
infusing matter with spirit across the plains
as rumbling thunder recedes to dark of East,
and above the land, stars glisten in the sky.
—"Thunder Beings," in *Cottonwood Moon* (1979), Richard F. Fleck

Some thirty years later, all winter long I anticipated our climb of sacred Harney Peak (7,242 feet), some 3,000 feet lower than Laramie Peak, but the highest point in South Dakota. Fortunately, during the winter I taught two classes that read *Black Elk Speaks* and other books relating to Lakota culture. *Black Elk Speaks* is a bi-autobiography* of Nicholas Black Elk, holy man of the Oglala Sioux, as told to John G. Neihardt in 1931. As Black Elk explains to Neihardt, "It is the story of all life that is holy and good to tell, and of us two-leggeds sharing in it with the four-leggeds and the wings of the air and all green things; for these are the children of one mother and their father is one Spirit."

At the very young age of nine, Black Elk, during sickness, was given a vision of harmony in which he was taken to the "center of the universe," being none other than Hin Han Kaga Paha or what we call Harney Peak in the heart of the Black Hills. There he was shown the "Flaming Rainbow Tipi," where six grandfathers showed him the way to harmonious living within a sacred hoop of the nation. Each of the six old men gave Black Elk a power to achieve this harmony, whether it was from the sacred North or East, South or West, or from the Sky above or the Earth below. It was very important that he listen with his heart and spirit to the old men, as bad times were coming to the Lakota people in which their spirit would be broken by they who were many, or the white men. Young Black Elk was given power to make live through thunder beings, the power to heal through the sacred herb, the power to make peace through the sacred pipe, the power to make whole through the flowering red stick, the power to transcend space through astral projection, and finally, the power to transcend time through maintaining the core of his youth even in old age. When the grandfathers left and the Flaming Rainbow Tipi disappeared, there stood Harney Peak. Black Elk and his people had a tough road to travel as they went through life from buffalo hunting to the battle with Custer, to Wounded Knee, and to reservation poverty, including the loss of the sacred Black Hills to gold miners and settlers. Not only had the Black Hills provided his people with food and water and tipi poles for shelter, they provided visions sought and visions given. Even though they became physically "owned" by gold miners and others, the Black Hills will always continue to nurture the Lakota spirit.

In late May, my wife, Maura, and I drove north by northeast to these "hills," with the intent of climbing Harney Peak, or Hin Han Kaga Paha, which translates roughly as "the sacred frightening owl," which must have served as a transmitter of a vision back in early times. I don't think I'll ever see again thunder beings of clouds so impressively metamorphic as those that gathered in a northwest to southeast line following the contour of South Dakota's Black Hills. I watched them as Maura and I drove from Lusk to Newcastle, Wyoming, on our way to meet our hiking companion at the Rapid City airport. Those puffy, white cumulus clouds shape-shifted from one type of being to another; an opened-beaked eagle, a lurching coyote, a rumbling buffalo, a sacred dancer with an arched back, an elderly man holding pointed hands above his ears all changed into something else. They all just hovered above the still invisible Black Hills, but you knew that those mountains had to be there because of their sky companions hovering above.

Meanwhile, our companion, John Borusheski, had just left his business meeting in Sacramento. An oh-so New Yorker at the meeting asked him, "So where is it you're flying to after here?"

John answered, "Rapid City."

"Oh," said the New Yorker, "I'm sorry."

We entered the hills whose dense stands of ponderosa pines had been recently blackened with forest fires—some two years ago (1998), some last year (2000). Buffalo grass grew back strong and softened the black soil with its gentle new growth. I looked up at the clouds, which now had become just clouds that layered the sky like ordinary clouds anywhere. Lush green meadows reminded Maura of her native Ireland. Windows lowered, we could catch the melodious notes of western meadowlarks, as rich as a thin sheet of hammer-tapped gold lining the altar of some Tibetan temple. These Black Hills began to tug at the psyche. They emanated some sort of invisible ray almost like the very visible fingers of pine-studded ridges connecting Laramie Peak and the old territorial Black Hills to these. Something more than cloud, geography, and mind came together here. We continued our drive through Custer, past the still-crude giant rock carving of Crazy Horse, through Hill City, past Mount Rushmore, and down to Rapid City and south to the airport. John's plane landed as we stood by a display case containing a Lakota headdress and other implements— the display case from the movie *Thunderheart*. John ambled along the walkway with other passengers—he was all smiles. We greeted one another and talked of Harney Peak. Maura pointed to it outside the airport. "Yes, I saw it out the plane window," he said.

We arose early on the next gray morning and proceeded back up into the Black Hills and Sylvan Lake. We hoped it wouldn't rain on us all the way up Harney Peak. We could hardly see Sylvan Lake; we only saw a bit of rocky shoreline. Mist hovered overhead, with the slightest droplets of fine rain sifting down from the faintly thundering sky. We shouldered our packs and talked of Black Elk. In 1931, the old Oglala holy man told poet John G. Neihardt, as he pointed toward Harney Peak, "There, when I was young, the spirits took me in my vision to the center of the earth and showed me all the good things in the sacred hoop of the world. I wish I could stand up there in the flesh before I die, for there is something I want to say to the six Grandfathers."

John, Maura, and I talked of the six Grandfathers representing East, South, West, North, Sky, and sacred Earth. Our feet touched the earth with each step we took up the gentle trail, scented with vanilla from the bark and sap of ponderosa pines. Although the sky remained heavy and overcast, distant notes of western song sparrows and white-crowned sparrows lent us some cheer. But the higher we rose through the woods, the brighter the sky became. The brightness of the sky was further accentuated on the ground by many sparkling, mica-coated rocks along the trail. We passed large, gray, overhanging boulders of granite and walked over to an open rocky ledge to the side of the woods, which afforded us a grand view eastward of granitic desert of badlands—a hobgoblin of rocks, some looking like shawled women, others like climbing turtles, and still others like perched owls. We noticed with joy that the sky had almost completely cleared, and a strong sun illuminated pine needles and rock as well as our inner spirits. Maura seemed delighted as she rambled along the trail with her walking stick.

John G. Neihardt helped arrange a trip to Harney Peak for Black Elk in 1931, as recorded in *Black Elk Speaks*. On the way up to the summit, the old man said to his son Ben, "Something should happen to-day. If I have any power left, the thunder beings of the west should hear me when I send a voice, and there should be at least a little thunder and a little rain." Black Elk's climb had begun under intensely blue skies. It was dry and warm. Thunderclouds seemed unlikely.

We continued upward past clusters of turtle rocks. Gradually, ponderosa pines received new neighbors of aspen and Douglas fir. Soft tufts of buffalo grass were pleasing to the eye. The trail rounded a corner and began to *descend*. We worried that we might be on the wrong trail. It descended past Indian shawl rocks farther and farther down toward soft green meadows. Along the way we paused to admire lush rock coatings of green moss. Irish green moss. But still the trail descended. We had real doubts that this was the right trail. What we needed, however, was patience. Soon we splashed through a stream and began to climb up through metamorphosed woods, now all lodgepole pines, so called for providing the Lakota people and others with tipi poles. While we hiked along in the warm sun, to the east and south it remained densely misted.

Black Elk and fellow climbers arrived atop a cloudless summit during a season of fierce drought—the historic drought of the early 1930s and Dust Bowl days. When he was a young man in the late 1870s, Black Elk went on a vision quest *(hamblechya)* and perched himself on one of the high, rocky domes atop Harney Peak (named after a US officer who arranged for the Lakota people to live on a reservation). He fasted and prayed for several days when a terrific thunderstorm approached him. Bolts of lightning forked the sky. Hailstones slanted down in sick, gray-green light toward young Black Elk. He thought for a moment he would be slashed to ribbons. But amazingly, the hail stopped just a few feet short of where he sat praying. Rumbling thunder slowly subsided. He knew he had been given the power of thunder beings. He would be a thunder-being person to serve his tribe during the encroachment of *wasichus* or "they who are many," who were coming from the east in search of gold and land and earthly power.

We proceeded higher through glistening lodgepole pines, with a few scattered higher-altitude spruce trees. Maura paused to point out a delightful view down the cliffs into a sunny wetland below. She told us to listen to the spring peepers. John and I stopped to listen to this peaceful woodland chorus. We all took swigs of canteen water, feeling as thirsty as buffalo who had wandered deep into the dry Badlands. As chipmunks scurried through the ground cover, we stopped once again, this time to listen to the distant piping of a Swainson's thrush from the forests below. And then we came upon it! Placed on a rock just below the final summit lay a beautiful Lakota prayer bundle, a cluster of flag cloths in six different colors: red for the rising sun of the east, yellow for the golden warmth of the south, black for the thunderheads of the west, white for the snows from the north, and a brilliant blue for the sky above, mated with chartreuse green for the sacred earth *(unci wakan)*—indeed, the Six Grandfathers. I sensed that the *wichasha wakan* (holy man) Black Elk would be happy looking down on this prayer bundle, making the *Paha Sapa* complete, even if the US government had failed to return these hills to the Lakota people to make amends for the broken Treaty of Fort Laramie.

We picked our way up the stone steps to the uppermost rocky summit of Harney Peak in the clear sunshine high above the veils of mist pushing up against the Black Hills from the east. On another rocky ridge just to the west—perhaps where young Black Elk sought his vision—stood a pure-white mountain goat with his black horns gleaming in the sun! The whole place emanated with energy. We felt like staying up here forever.

As we ate some trail mix and looked into the six directions, another hiker named Gary joined us at the summit. He had moved out to South Dakota from the crowds of the East. He had lived here in the Black Hills for ten years. John asked him what he thought of Mount Rushmore and the Crazy Horse Monument. He said, "I guess I'm old-fashioned. I like things the way they were a hundred years ago. To me, it's wrong to deface Nature by carving anything into these rocks. Let them be. They are, after all, held sacred by the native people."

I asked him what he liked about the Black Hills. "Oh, I guess I like their beauty, their eagles, the increasing number of mountain lions. I think there are around 300 of them now in the Black Hills. I like the white-tailed deer and the mule deer. I don't know, these hills are a self-sustaining piece of terrain on this tired old planet."

"What do you think about the native people?"

"I think," he said, "they are coming back stronger. Have you ever been to Bear Butte or Devil's Tower? They've placed prayer bundles and prayer flags all around them. That's beginning to say something—that there's more than gold in them thar hills."

We all listened to him intently. Maura looked particularly pensive.

Old Black Elk dressed and painted himself in the presence of John G. Neihardt and Ben Black Elk. As recorded in *Black Elk Speaks,* he exclaimed, "Hey-a-a-hey! Hey-a-a-hey! Hey-a-a-hey, Hey-a-a-hey! Grandfather, Great Spirit, once more behold me on earth and lean to hear my feeble voice. . . . All things belong to you—two-leggeds, the four-leggeds, the wings of the air and all green things that live. You have set the powers of the four quarters to cross each other. . . . Therefore I am sending you a voice, Great Spirit, my Grandfather, forgetting nothing you have made, the stars of the universe and the grasses of the earth." He continued to implore the Great Spirit, Tongashula, to listen to his prayer to make the earth whole again and his people whole again (especially, I might add, after the devastation of the Wounded Knee Massacre in 1890, the misery and buffalo-less-poverty, living in square, wooden homes on a reservation arranged by General Harney, and right then in 1931, the blasting and carving of American presidents' faces out of sacred rock). As the old man continued his supplications to Tongashula, thin rain clouds gathered and a "scant chill rain" fell from seemingly out of nowhere. Black Elk prayed, "In sorrow I am sending a feeble voice, O Six Powers of the World. Hear me in my sorrow, for I may never call again. O make my people live!"

Indeed, we thought to ourselves as we stood atop the highest point of land east of the Rockies in North America. While the national forests, including this Black Elk Wilderness Area, still remain under the control of the US government, it is not too late for officials to sign a revitalized document representing a final peace to a people. Let their prayer bundles come true. Amid this mystic piping of spring peepers from lower vales, we said our good-byes to our fellow climber and wished him well. We made our descent from Harney Peak down to the green and rolling prairies and somewhat reluctantly toward our respective homes. We hoped that at very least the government should return a small wild portion of the Black Hills (such as the Black Elk Wilderness Area) to the Lakota people as a symbolic gesture of goodwill.

III—Black Elk's Prayer Atop Harney Peak

I discovered this hitherto unpublished prayer among John G. Neihardt's papers (not included in his *Black Elk Speaks,* 1932) in the W. W. Thompson Folklore Collection at the New York State Historical Association in Cooperstown. I quote John G. Neighardt: "Black Elk's words, spoken in Sioux, as translated by his son [Ben], taken in shorthand by John Neihardt's daughter, and finally reported by the poet himself. . . . [It was] spoken atop a high hill [Harney Peak] in the emptiness of the great plains, [where Nicolas Black Elk] faced west, the power that makes life and that destroys.

> Grandfather, great mysterious one. You have been always, and before you nothing has been. There is nothing to pray but to you. The star nations all over the universe are yours, and yours are the grasses of the earth. Day in and day out you are the life of things. You are older than all need, older than all pain and prayer.
>
> Grandfather, all over the world the faces of living ones are alike. In tenderness they have come up out of the ground. Look upon your children with children in their arms that they may face the winds and walk the good road to the day of quiet.
>
> Teach me to walk the soft earth a relative to all that live. Sweeten my heart and fill me with light. Give me the strength to understand and the eyes to see. Help me for without you I am nothing.
> [1931].

(With permission of the New York State Historical Association)

* As-told-to biography

18

MOUNTAINS OVER
THE DESERT

Late in August the lure of the mountains becomes irresistible. Seared by the everlasting sunfire, I want to see running water again, embrace a pine tree, cut my initials in the bark of an aspen, get bit by a mosquito, see a mountain bluebird, find a big blue columbine, get lost in the firs, hike above timberline, sunbathe on snow and eat some ice, climb the rocks and stand in the wind at the top of the world on the peak of Tukuhnikivats.

—Edward Abbey, *Desert Solitaire*

I REMEMBER FIRST going to Arches National Monument with my father after we both had read Abbey's classic *Desert Solitaire* a few weeks after it was published in 1968. I still have the original hardcover first edition. We got up at three o'clock in the morning and left Laramie for the town of Dinosaur, Colorado. As tempting as it was to stop and explore Dinosaur National Monument, we continued driving south on a rolling desert road to Grand Junction and westward to Moab. The arches formations looked exactly as Abbey had described them—a fantastic array of orange sandstone fins suspended in midair and gigantic chess pieces balancing precariously high above scrub junipers and pinyon pines. Soon my father and I hoofed along the trail to the Delicate Arch under cobalt-blue skies with tiny ripples of cloud. As the trail gained elevation up over slickrock, we both had the distinct impression that this was Mars; the bright orange-red soil lent credence to our impression. But yucca, prickly pear cactus, desert poppies, and scraggly sagebrush convinced us otherwise, unless we tramped over a Martian landscape now rich in oxygen.

We stopped to drink some water and eat peanut-butter sandwiches and chips. A desert wren flicked past us, and a pinyon jay, as blue as the sky, perched itself on a pine branch above our heads. We climbed to the top of a high mound of sandstone overlooking miles of desert. At one point, we edged along a narrow cliff until we rounded the far side of it to be afforded a fine view of Delicate Arch perched, as delicately as the pinyon jay, above a plateau of wrinkled orange sandstone.

Approaching the arch, we could see ever so clearly the mountains over the desert—the La Sal Range—rising, snowcapped, in the distance. The Spanish explorer Frey Francisco Silvestre Velez de Escalante named the mountains "La Sal," thinking they must be covered with salt, not snow. How could it be otherwise in such a hot desert? The name has stuck ever since. Their name may, after all, be quite apt. Ten million years ago, the La Sals were formed by inner volcanic uplifting of much older collapsed salt deposits to form giant, unbroken blisters called laccoliths, through which no volcanic materials extruded. These laccoliths gradually gained their prominent shape through millions of years of erosion and glaciation to become spectacular mountains above the desert.

We ended our journey at a point where Delicate Arch framed those mountains. White snow and desert heat! Stark and empty foreground and wispy white mountains in the background. Yes, my father and I could see why Edward Abbey needed to climb up and out of the desert to a pinnacle of rock in celestial space. They are an amazing biogeographic island in the desert on which grow a unique species of flower—the rayless daisy *(Erigeron mancus)*—found nowhere else on the planet. It would be thirty-five years later that I, too, would experience this unique alpine island.

The La Sals are second to the Uintas in height in the state of Utah. They are a relatively short range, being only fifteen miles long and a mere six miles wide, just east of Moab. There are more than ten peaks above 12,000 feet, with Mount Peale being the tallest at 12,721 feet, among the highest in Utah. The other peaks have an array of colorful names: Tukuhnikivats (where the sun lingers in Ute), Talking Mountain, Tomasaki, Mellenthin (pronounced melon-teen), and, on the east side, Mount Waas. They are usually blanketed with snow (not salt) from November to April and the highest of the La Sals sparkle with snow well into July. They, like the Uintas, have lush forests of lodgepole pines, aspen, spruce, and fir. It is quite a pleasure to the eye to see them from a raft in the Colorado River north of Moab near Fisher Towers, but even more pleasant to be up in them.

Michael Mackey (of fish-cave fame on Mount Princeton) and I sat in our folding camp chairs with mugs of tea late in the day in a high alpine meadow above Geyser Pass. We were looking across the way to Mount Mellenthin, which was catching the dying rays of sun. Although the marsh mosquitoes of late June buzzed our ears, nothing could disturb us as we watched a dark shadow creep across the western flank of Mellenthin—we could see the shadow slowly move across upper scree of that mountain, now covering a partially lit rock with total darkness. As the sun sank below the western horizon of a golden desert far below, Mellenthin began to turn from dark gray to rosy pink. It was pure alpine theater, and no buzzing mosquitoes or fluttering millers could break the spell. Slivers of upper snowfields appeared to have become huge slices of watermelon; white-throated sparrows added musical accompaniment to the show. And then, as our meadow darkened in the chill of an early summer evening in the La Sals, the entire western sky glimmered with an alpine glow.

Getting up here to set up camp certainly wasn't as pleasantly cool as this evening. After witnessing miles on end of bushless dirt mounds and dry washes along Interstate 70, we turned off at the Cisco, Utah, exit and headed toward the Colorado River and the distant La Sal Mountains, which loomed like phantoms above the desert. The closer we got to the canyon of the Colorado River, the denser the desert vegetation became, including sagebrush, rabbitbrush, and thickening groves of sweet-smelling tamarisk. It was such a relief to finally drive along the shorelines of the churning and thrashing Colorado River. We followed the river for a dozen miles or so until we entered Castle Valley, with the bright red Fisher Towers and a series of buttes called the Professor Rocks looking like giant human figures cowled in graduation robes. At last the La Sal Loop Road!

Ever upward, we climbed past tamarisk and juniper bushes and pinyon pines, which then yielded to extensive groves of scrub-oak trees rustling in the dry desert winds. Ravens circled the skies above while riding the thermal layers of air. And then came lush groves of tall, graceful aspen trees. Somewhere near an elevation of 7,000 feet, we turned onto a steep gravel road leading skyward toward Geyser Pass at 9,500 feet. Beyond the aspen groves, we entered dense forests of Douglas fir, Engelmann spruce, and subalpine fir. My, how cool it had become as we stood outside the car at Geyser Pass, scanning the meadows for the ruts of a four-wheel-drive road. We discovered several sets of ruts but chose a pair that led northward toward the flanks of Haystack Mountain, looming above the pass. Finding an ideal spot for our campsite at 10,000 feet, we pulled over and unloaded our gear.

We talked of Edward Abbey later that evening as we sat around a nice crackling fire. He certainly got relief up here from that hot desert sun in Arches National Monument, as it was called in those days. In fact, it felt like Ed was with us that night, although we had forgotten to bring an after-dinner bottle of German wine to share with him. Abbey drove his jeep up to about this altitude forty years earlier, just below the talus-laden slopes of steep Mount Tukuhnikivats. In the chilly air, after supper, he laid out his bedroll, which was still warm from the desert below, and soon dreamed of his ascent the next day. Abbey, at that time, was thirty-five years younger than I was, and my stamina for several thousand feet of loose talus slopes had diminished considerably. Not that a much younger

Michael and I would not experience loose and sliding rocks the next day! We both believed that Abbey was a remarkable person and a remarkable writer. But clearly, he was a much better essayist than he was a novelist, and clearly, we reflected that night, *Desert Solitaire* remains a classic to this day. I told Michael of another friend of mine from Japan who was also an Abbey aficionado. He had planned to translate *Desert Solitaire* into Japanese. But, as he said, the title alone proved to be as difficult a challenge as the loose scree of Tukuhnikivats. How do you get into Japanese the double meaning of the words "desert solitaire?" That is, to play a philosophical game of solitaire, not with cards, but with the desert, and at the same time, to live and think in solitude (not loneliness) in the desert. By the time Professor Minoru Fujita, a leading Shakespearean scholar, thought he might be ready to start translating, he was beaten to the punch, but the Japanese edition that did get published had a totally unsatisfactory translation of the title *Desert Solitaire*.

On that hot August day, Edward Abbey needed the yin of the snowy La Sal Mountains to balance the yang of sandstone fins shimmering in heat waves above Salt Creek. After he woke up at dawn at his mountain campsite, he ate a quick breakfast and bounded up the loose talus, sometimes slipping, certainly sweating and grunting, and eventually standing on the high summit of Tukuhnikivats, looking down on the shimmering desert heat of endless miles of red sandstone and alkaline flats and seemingly Mars itself. What a fine haiku of contrast— snow, chilly air, alpine granite, squeaking pikas, and rosy finches fluttering above tree line so far above searing, dry heat, hazy dust, cactus, Spanish bayonet, yucca, pinyon jays, and parched, sandy soil!

I slept outside that night near the glowing embers of our campfire. The insects had calmed down, and the stars seemed to swirl across the black sky like Vincent Van Gogh's *Starry Night*. I listened to the symphony of white-crowned sparrows in the surrounding woods and heard the footfall of mule deer grazing in the meadow where Michael and I watched the great alpine theater on Mount Mellenthin. A meteor flashed across the sky with a green streak. I dozed off again for another hour or so until four o'clock in the morning, when mosquitoes began to buzz through the air, along with clumsy millers. It was chilly—mighty chilly. I pulled the cord of the sleeping bag tight to mummify myself, and I dozed off again for another hour or so until I heard a fantastic symphony of song sparrows, white-crowned sparrows, and Swainson's thrushes: *Mc vie a doo, mc vie a doo, A-tee-tee-tee-tee, A myrtle, a turtle, a wurtle, Mc vie a doo.* Again a clumsy miller brushed past my ear. I had to get up. It was dawn. Indeed, there is more day to dawn, as Thoreau exclaims. I walked out to the meadow to witness a different alpine show. Mount Mellenthin caught the eastern rays of an unrisen sun (from my standpoint) and began to glow with a bright tangerine color. Mule deer pranced below me, and an eagle sailed above. I walked back to the camp and lit a burner to make some coffee. Michael began to stir inside his tent. In minutes, we both stood around a stick fire made from the still-glowing embers of last night and drank coffee between bites of breakfast bars. Now was the time to pack for our climb of nearby Haystack Mountain.

We followed a trail through a spruce and fir forest until we emerged into a bright meadow blanketed with chiming bells, alpine avens, red-berried alder, and prickly squaw currant bushes. After building a small cairn of rocks atop a flat stone to mark our return trail, we aimed our way toward Haystack Mountain, which rose to our left just above tree line. We walked across hardened pocket-gopher mud grooves that earlier served as tunnels through deep snow. What busy creatures they are. Crossing several trickling and icy rivulets fingering their way through marshy ground, we approached a high grove of spruce trees just below a 300- or 400-foot-high slope of loose talus framing the blue sky. At this elevation, in the Colorado Mountains, one would find numerous twisted and weathered limber pines, but none here. There is no such tree in the isolated La Sals. This range of mountains is so isolated from similar high mountains, that a unique biogeographic zone evolved through the millennia. Such isolation allowed for the lack of common alpine species like the limber pine, and it also allowed for the evolution of unique species like the rayless daisy. Arriving at the base of talus, we sat down for a rest, munched on some trail mix, and took swigs of orange Gatorade. We leaned over to admire delicate clusters of purple alpine forget-me-nots, deep pink Parry's primroses, and white moss campion, and looked all around us for the unique rayless daisy—but saw nary a one. It remained pleasantly cool so high above Moab. We both wondered if Abbey had not sought the relief of the La Sals more often than he wrote about. I know I sure as hell would have. But then, my ranger days were served high in Rocky Mountain National Park, not Arches, so perhaps I would need the La Sals more than Abbey did. I recalled the time when I traveled through the Utah and Arizona deserts headed toward the Grand Canyon while still a ranger in Colorado. I so missed my Colorado Rockies when I was out there in the grease-wood flats of the desert. And then the road began to climb up out of Kanab out of the desert into the fresh, lush forests of the Kaibab Plateau. It was nice to be back in the aspen and spruce. As I write this, just two weeks ago, we traveled that same rising road up to the Kaibab Plateau with friends from France. Jean-Louis Picherit remarked to me that he "never expected the approach to the North Rim of the Grand Canyon to be as lushly forested as this!"

Like Abbey, we, too, began our cautious ascent of loose and treacherous talus slabs formed by millions of years of freeze and thaw and thaw and freeze. They seemed to be like a very slow-moving glacier of rocks. But they can move fast, all right. I crept upslope carefully and slowly, more slowly than Michael, who climbed ten or fifteen yards higher than I did. Not as much lichen on those wobbly rocks as their equivalents in the Colorado Rockies! I looked up and there stood Michael, all smiles, on a false summit of Haystack Mountain. A minute or two later, after several zigzags, I joined Michael and stood and stared into the vast space of the lower desert. Michael pointed toward the higher cairns marking the summit of Haystack Mountain, and we proceeded along the flat rocks and onto a gently rising snowfield leading toward the summit. We gingerly crossed several smaller snowfields and stood at the summit to look southward at a not-so-high Mellenthin and the much higher Tukuhnikivats, Talking Mountain, and Mount Peale, the highest of the La Sal Range, rising not quite to 13,000 feet. We checked our wind-torn map to find the names of peaks to the north: Tomasaki, Manns, and La Sal. Snowcapped peaks and shimmering desert make for a La Sal experience.

Abbey, feeling the need to return to desert reality, selected a Tukuhnikivats snowfield, tested it by throwing a flat rock on it to see how fast it would go, and soon followed the rock down a flank of Tukuhnikivats somewhat too fast. Fortunately, he came to a roaring halt just before some sharp, jagged rocks. All too soon he turned on the ignition of his vehicle to drive back down to a desert ignited with furnace heat. What is desert reality? Abbey explains just why he chose the desert: "I am here not only to evade for a while the clamor and filth and confusion of the cultural apparatus but also to confront, immediately and directly, if it's possible, the bare bones of existence, the elemental and fundamental, the bedrock which sustains us."

We weren't quite ready to make our descent because we didn't have a descending snowfield to lower depths as an option. We ate more trail mix and continued to enjoy the view of mountains above the desert. From here, at 11,641 feet, we could clearly discern how narrow this range of mountains is. From Geyser Pass, they immediately sloped downward both east and west, with just a narrow ridge between. They were only six miles wide—truly an island in the desert.

We began our descent back across the snowfields to the very edge of the false summit overlooking a steep slope of loose talus. Michael started first and I followed, being careful not to be exactly above him in case I caused a rock or two to slide down. At one point, halfway down, a rock I stood upon started to slide a few inches, causing me to sit down rather abruptly. From this position I stared at tiny dots of shining cars creeping along the La Sal Loop Road far below. A lone jet streaked across the sky, creating a vapor trail. Not many jet routes cross the La Sal Range—perhaps this jet was en route to Las Vegas from Minneapolis. I cautiously arose and proceeded with many mountain goat zig-zags through the scree down to the meadow below, where Michael sat eating an energy bar. We high-fived it after I made it down. Again I looked for the elusive rayless daisy, with no luck. I wished that the one and only guidebook for the La Sals had, at the very least, a picture of this flower—that might have helped, perhaps.

After we passed through the small stand of Engelmann spruce, we looked down at several meadows, not knowing which meadow might be the correct one for our return trail. I suggested sticking to a higher contour line and following it for a half mile around to a large meadow. But once we arrived there, it didn't look right. Oh, for a GPS! Three or four meadows lay far below. Which one should we go to? For a moment I was reminded of my early ranger experience, when I ascended Mount Ida from Lake Julian in Rocky Mountain National Park fifty years ago, only to look down on three lakes, not just one. I wondered which one was Lake Julian since they all looked alike. My friends awaited me with a nice packed lunch. Of course, I chose the wrong lake on my return journey. I paid for my mistake with eighteen hours of tramping through trailless twisting valleys to the Colorado River and civilization.

Here in Utah, we rapidly descended to a lower meadow, but it wasn't the right one! Michael suggested going through an aspen grove and hopefully coming out at the right spot. What had we to lose? We came out at the wrong meadow. In the worse-case scenario, we could freelance it down to Geyser Pass right under Mount Mellenthin and hike back up the four-wheel-drive road to our campsite. Instead, we proceeded southwesterly through another aspen grove to see, at last, our cairn above a meadow trail. All too soon we arrived back at the campsite, broke camp, and drove down to Geyser Pass and to the lower La Sal Loop Road. Like Edward Abbey, we descended to the heat of Moab for a most refreshing lunch. Out on the streets of Moab again, stunned by the heat, we looked up at the snow-streaked La Sal Mountains, wondering if we had ever been there. Were they mere phantoms of the mind? The desert can do things to you like that.

EPILOGUE:
A ROCK ON MY DESK

I HAVE ON MY desk a compressed piece of white sandstone with just a bit of red sandstone still clinging to the bottom edge. Perhaps this sandstone rolled down from the upper cliffs of Split Mountain Gorge to the Green River shoreline where I picked it up from the beach not far from my sleeping bag. I would guess that it is a piece of Weber sandstone, but whatever it is, this old rock, held in my hand, brings back youthful memories.

Just south of the three-corner area where Utah, Wyoming, and Colorado meet, lies Dinosaur National Monument. Here the Green and Yampa Rivers join at Steamboat Rock to flow south hundreds of miles all the way to the Colorado River. This grand confluence of rivers is in Canyonlands National Park south of Moab, Utah. The rivers within Dinosaur National Monument have cut deep into the 150 million-year-old Morrison Formation of the Jurassic Period when dinosaurs roamed. Thousands of dinosaur skeletons have been exposed as a result of river action.

As a young bachelor back in 1959, I wished to explore this National Monument by driving west of Maybell, Colorado, to follow a winding dirt road for thirty-five miles toward the entrance way of the Yampa River into the

eastern canyon of red, rocky cliffs. I remember passing a sign with a warning—4-WHEEL DRIVE ONLY BEYOND THIS POINT! Not to be deterred, I continued over jutting rocks and potholes until my 1950 light green Ford felt like
it was going to split in half, like the canyon. Suddenly two ruts the size of small
ditches filled with water quickly appeared ahead. I backed up my nine-year-old
car, got up speed, and skidded through muddy ditches at forty-five miles per
hour. I almost lost it but roared like a stegosaur out onto hard sand and drove
up into a cottonwood grove beneath bloody red cliffs where the Yampa River
enters Dinosaur National Monument. All kinds of cactus bloomed with strawberry red blossoms, something I had never seen before.

Despite the gnawing worry of getting back out to the main road (US 40),
I became entranced by the immensity of the hollow depths ahead of me and the
echoing sounds of ravens cawing deep within the canyon—or were they Triassic
pterodactyls? I couldn't help but notice the rich variety of cacti growing all
around me: prickly pear cactus with yellow blossoms, pincushion cactus with
pink blossoms, and, of course, strawberry cactus. Suddenly a disturbing rumbling sound grew louder and louder—my first thought was that an earthquake
was about to take place. But when I saw a flank of inner canyon lit up by lightning for a split second, I knew a prehistoric thunderstorm was about to explode
around me. My only hope was to leave immediately this enchanted place without the slightest hesitation.

As I backed up my car, thunder boomed and echoed deep within Yampa
Canyon sounding as though a multispecies battle of dinosaurs had begun.
If ever I felt like a modern intruder in ancient times, it was then. This time I
had a level one hundred yards to gain speed and easily (well not too easily)
splashed through the muddy ditches that were pelted with tiny drops of misty
rain from the approaching storm. I succeeded in outrunning the storm and
arrived at the good old hardtop road to continue on to Vernal, Utah, and the
Green River campgrounds.

Before coming to Dinosaur National Monument, I had read John Wesley
Powell's *Exploration of the Colorado River and Its Canyons* (1895) in which he

describes his 1867 exploratory expedition of the Colorado: "Lying down, we look up through the canyon and see that only a little of the blue heaven appears overhead—a crescent of blue sky, with two or three constellations peering down upon us. I do not sleep for some time, as the excitement of the day has not worn off. Soon I see a bright star that appears to rest on the very verge of the cliff overhead to the east. Slowly it seems to float from its resting place on the rock over the canyon. . . . I almost wonder that it does not fall."

That evening, I slept outdoors where the Green River exits the canyon. I, too, could hardly get to sleep after the excitement of the day. Stars floated in the sky. I finally fell asleep seemingly to wake up minutes later at sunrise to see the cliffs illuminated so brilliantly I thought I was in some other kind of world.

A Selective Reading List of Informative Mountain and Desert Books

Abbey, Edward. *Desert Solitaire.* New York: McGraw-Hill, 1968.

Barcott, Bruce. *The Measure of a Mountain: Beauty and Terror on Mount Rainier.* Seattle: Sasquatch Books, 1997.

Bird, Isabella. *A Lady's Life in the Rocky Mountains.* New York: Putnam's Sons, 1879.

Blackstock, Alan, ed. *A Green River Reader.* Salt Lake City: University of Utah Press, 2005.

Childs, Craig. *House of Rain: Tracking a Vanished Civilization Across the American Southwest.* Boston: Back Bay Books, 2008.

Dolnick, Edward. *Down the Great Unknown: John Wesley Powell's 1869 Journey of Discovery and Tragedy through the Grand Canyon.* New York: Harper-Collins, 2001.

Douglas, William O. *Of Men and Mountains: The Classic Memoir of Wilderness Adventure.* New York: Harper and Row, 1950.

Evans-Wentz, W. Y. *Cuchama and Sacred Mountains.* Athens: Swallow Press/University of Ohio Press, 1989.

Fergusson, Erna. *Dancing Gods: Indian Ceremonials of New Mexico and Arizona.* Albuquerque: The University of New Mexico Press, 1931.

Fleck, Richard F. *A Colorado River Reader.* Salt Lake City: University of Utah Press, 2000.

Fletcher, Colin. *A Thousand Mile Summer.* Berkeley: Howell-North Books, 1964.

Frick, Thomas. *The Sacred Theory of Earth.* Berkeley: North Atlantic Books, 1986.

Graham, Stephen. *Tramping with a Poet in the Rockies.* New York: Appleton and Company, 1922.

Kent, Rockwell. *Wilderness: A Journal of Quiet Adventure in Alaska.* New York: Modern Library, 1920.

Knighton, Jose. *Canyon Country's La Sal Mountains: Hiking and Nature Handbook.* Moab: Canyon Country Publications, 1995.

Krakauer, Jon. *Eiger Dreams: Ventures Among Men and Mountains.* New York: Farrar, Straus and Giroux, 1997.

McPhee, John. *Rising from the Plains.* New York: Farrar, Straus and Giroux, 1987.

Meloy, Ellen. *Raven's Exile: A Season on the Green River.* Tucson: University of Arizona Press, 2003.

Mills, Enos A. *The Rocky Mountain Wonderland.* Boston: Houghton Mifflin, 1915.

Mitchell, Finis. *Wind River Trails: A Hiking and Fishing Guide.* Salt Lake City: Wasatch Publishers, 1975.

Momaday, N. Scott. *The Way to Rainy Mountain.* Albuquerque: The University of New Mexico Press, 1968.

Muir, John. *Mountaineering Essays,* ed. Richard F. Fleck. Salt Lake City: University of Utah Press, 1997.

Neihardt, John G. *Black Elk Speaks,* with introduction by Vine Deloria, Jr. Lincoln: University of Nebraska Press, 1997 reprint of 1932 edition.

Norgay, Jamling Tenzing. *Touching My Father's Soul: A Sherpa's Journey to the Top of Everest.* San Francisco: HarperCollins, 2001.

O'Brien, Dan. *Buffalo for the Broken Heart: Restoring Life to a Black Hills Ranch.* New York: Random House, 2002.

Powell, John Wesley. *Exploration of the Colorado River and Its Canyons.* New York: Flood & Vincent, 1895, reprinted in paperback by Dover Publications, 1961.

Preston, Douglas. *Talking to the Ground: One Family's Journey on Horseback Across the Sacred Land of the Navajo.* Albuquerque: The University of New Mexico Press, 1995.

Rusho, W. L. *The Mystery of Everett Ruess.* Salt Lake City: Gibbs Smith, 2010. (This is a revised edition of *Everett Ruess, A Vagabond for Beauty,* 1982.)

Saner, Reg. *Reaching Keet Seel: Ruin's Echo & the Anasazi.* Salt Lake City: University of Utah Press, 1998.

Silko, Leslie Marmon. *Ceremony.* New York: Viking, 1977.

Worster, Donald. *A River Running West: The Life of John Wesley Powell.* New York: Oxford University Press, 2001. (See pages 147–149, Powell's route up Longs Peak.)

Zwinger, Ann H. *Wind in the Rock: The Canyonlands of Southeastern Utah.* Tucson: University of Arizona Press, 1978.

Note: I decided to provide first edition information simply because many of these books have multiple reprint editions.

About the Author

Richard Francis Fleck was born in Philadelphia, Pennsylvania, in 1937 and is the author or editor of a number of books: scholarly and creative nonfiction, fiction, and poetry. His scholarly works include *Henry Thoreau and John Muir Among the Indians* (Archon Books, 1985), *Critical Perspectives on Native American Fiction* (Three Continents Press, 1993), and an online edition of *The Indians of Thoreau: Selections from the Indian Notebooks* (The Thoreau Institute at Walden Woods, 2007) that was originally published by Hummingbird Press in 1974. He edited and introduced a number of trade paperback editions of Thoreau, Muir, and Burroughs and has written two novels and a number of small press collections of poems, the latest being *Mountains on My Mind* (Amazon Kindle Book, 2013).

He attended Rutgers University where he received a B.A. in French (1959), Colorado State University where he received an M.A. in English (1962), and the University of New Mexico where he received a Ph.D in English (1970). He has taught American literature and Native American literature at the University of Wyoming, the State University of New York at Cortland, Osaka University, Japan, and the University of Bologna, Italy. He is an avid hiker of prairies, deserts, and mountains along with his wife, Maura, three children, Rich, Michelle, and Maureen, and their families, which include seven grandchildren.

In 2002 he received NEH recognition for his book *A Colorado River Reader* (University of Utah Press, 2000) that was selected as the discussion book for a seven-state project called Moving Waters: The Colorado River and the West. His favorite writers are Henry David Thoreau, John Muir, Willa Cather, N. Scott Momaday, Edward Abbey, and Leslie Marmon Silko. His favorite national park is Rocky Mountain National Park where he served as a seasonal ranger naturalist from 1959 to 1961.

A Note on This Edition

Breaking Through the Clouds first came out in 2004 and was very well received by regional journals and newspapers. But, over the years, I felt the need to expand this edition to include counterpoint experiences in the desert, canyon lands, and dry prairie far below the summits of the lofty peaks of the intermountain West. I decided to delete two chapters from the 2004 edition that had nothing to do with the intermountain West: "Asian and Alaskan Interludes," and "A New England Interlude." My literary model for attempting to depict the counterpoint of mountain and desert was Edward Abbey's *Desert Solitaire*, especially when he describes his urgent need to escape the furnace heat of Arches in August by climbing all the way up to the snowy summit of Tukuhnikivats, rising 9,000 feet above shimmering desert heat. In so doing, he succeeded in involving his readers with an equally potent but different kind of natural reality. After all, do not western mountains rise out of deserts and dry lands? Mountains and surrounding deserts should not be separated.

Index